"As you'll see in this amazing new book, gratitude is a mental state that a) you can easily decide to feel, b) has the most immediate effect on improving your well-being, and c) is going to have a remarkable impact on your ability to lead other people."

—Marshall Goldsmith, *New York Times* bestselling author
of *What Got You Here Won't Get You There*

"Seeing and appreciating excellence is foundational in running a great team, and yet so few leaders have mastered this seemingly simple skill. *Leading with Gratitude* is a powerful, poignant road map that can lead you and your team to extraordinary results."

—Amy Edmondson, professor, Harvard Business School,
and author of *The Fearless Organization* and *Teaming*

"All over the world, business leaders wait for the next insights from Adrian Gostick and Chester Elton. In this timely book, they show how the power of gratitude can supercharge results and transform organizations. I'm grateful they wrote it; you'll be grateful to read it."

—Henry Timms, president of Lincoln Center for the
Performing Arts, coauthor of *New Power*,
and cofounder of #GivingTuesday

"This brilliant book will disrupt the way you think about leading people. Carefully researched, witty, and packed with a hundred practical tips, *Leading with Gratitude* is a blueprint to developing your soft skills. Gratitude—essential for sustaining warm, productive relationships in all human endeavors—can't be coat-checked at the office door. It's a hallmark of a great business culture, not a superfluous nicety. Kudos to Gostick and Elton, the undisputed thought leaders in building All In cultures, for turning a spotlight on the under-practiced virtue of workplace gratitude."

—Whitney Johnson, founder and CEO of WLJ Advisors, and award-winning author of *Disrupt Yourself* and *Build an A-Team*

"Another instant classic by Gostick and Elton. Learning how to 'lead with gratitude' is a core business competency, and this book should be required reading for all people leaders. An exceptionally inspired workforce will respond in kind."

—David Kasiarz, executive vice president of Global Total Rewards and Medical, American Express

"This is *the* book people will be talking about this year. A powerful and profound method to inspire people to rally to your cause and achieve outstanding long-term results. Jam packed with ideas and tips to engage the people in your care, this book should be in every leader's library."

—Lance Trenary, president and CEO of Golden Corral Corporation

"Rooted in profound theory, nurtured by rigorous research, and illustrated by moving stories, Gostick and Elton turn the ideal of gratitude into a vibrant, flourishing, and renewing lifestyle. Their remarkable work will inspire and improve anyone from senior leader to frontline employee in any setting where we work, live, play, and worship."

—Dave Ulrich, Rensis Likert Collegiate
Professor of Business Administration,
University of Michigan, and partner at The RBL Group

"I love how this book uses hard data to explain that it is the soft stuff that makes all the difference for great leaders. Then, through benchmarking great leaders, it provides relevant and actionable ideas for how to make gratitude a sustainable force for good. As you'll see, authentic gratitude can change lives and change companies."

—Mark A. Beck, CEO of B-Square Precision Group

"Research has clearly shown that the best leaders positively engage with their people consistently. *Leading with Gratitude* hits at the essence and continued rebirth of what it is to be a leader. If you want sustained performance, hire leaders who possess 'power skills' like gratitude. The research in this book shows that people drive performance; leaders who understand this—and routinely show appreciation and gratitude for work and effort—will drive even more business!"

—Todd Billingsley, director of Business and
Leadership Development, Boehringer Ingelheim

"Gostick and Elton have captured the extraordinary essence of a driving life force to grow every sustainable organization. This book inspires, provokes, encourages, and serves as a launching pad for that next level of performance of your team, your company, and your community!"

—Mark C. Thompson, *New York Times* bestselling leadership author and #1 ranked CEO coach

Leading with Gratitude

Leading

with

Gratitude

Eight Leadership Practices for Extraordinary Business Results

Adrian Gostick
Chester Elton

HARPER
BUSINESS

An Imprint of HarperCollinsPublishers

HarperCollins books may be purchased for educational, business, or sales promotional use. For information, please email the Special Markets Department at SPsales@harpercollins.com.

FIRST EDITION

Library of Congress Cataloging-in-Publication Data has been applied for.

ISBN 978-0-06-296578-3

20 21 22 23 24   LSC   10 9 8 7 6 5 4 3 2 1

To Marshall Goldsmith,
who made this book possible

Contents

PART II: THE EIGHT MOST POWERFUL
GRATITUDE PRACTICES

Seeing

Expressing

PART III: A GRATEFUL LIFE

Foreword

have flown eleven million miles on American Airlines alone, not to mention one million on British Airways. The airplane is a fascinating place to watch people become agitated over factors they cannot hope to impact. One trigger that makes a lot of people crazy is the announcement that the airplane is going to be late.

Every time I hear that particular announcement, I remember a picture in my library—a picture of me on a volunteer trip to Africa with the Red Cross when I was about thirty years old. With me are many starving children whose arms are being measured. If their arms were too big, they did not eat. If their arms were too small, they did not eat. Their arms had to be just the right size, meaning they were not too hungry to survive and not too well fed so as not to need food. Their arm size determined whether they would eat that day.

I will never forget that experience. It reminds me daily of how fortunate I am. When I feel "justifiably" upset, I remember those beautiful children. I repeat this mantra over and over in my mind: "Never complain because the airplane is late. There are people in the world who have real problems.

They have problems you cannot even begin to imagine. Be grateful. You are a very lucky man. Never complain because the airplane is late."

I hope that someday this story helps you turn a moment of pain and anger into a moment of gratitude and joy.

Lots of people struggle with a lack of gratitude. And everyone I've ever met—whether a janitor or a billionaire—wants a happy life. No matter who you are, you can easily look for happiness in the wrong place. The great Western disease is "I'll be happy when." When I make a certain amount of money, get an award, or complete some task, I'll be happy.

What we can all learn is how vital gratitude is for our happiness. The wisest and happiest people I have met—Thich Nhat Hanh, the Dalai Lama, and others—talk about, and practice, deep gratitude. What I notice when I talk with them is how freely they express it. Allowing yourself to feel deeply grateful is how you can do something bold. Be happy now. Not later.

As you'll see in this amazing new book from Adrian Gostick and Chester Elton, gratitude is a mental state that a) you can most easily decide to feel, b) has the most immediate effect on improving your well-being, and c) is going to have a remarkable impact on your ability to lead other people. The challenge is to remember to do it!

It's important to create triggers in your work and in your life to remember to focus on gratitude. That's what my friends Adrian and Chester introduce in this book. Their lessons are fun to read, on point, and relevant for every manager, parent, coach, spouse, or partner to be able to put gratitude to work in their work and their lives.

The key to a happy life isn't what people think. It's not wealth, fame, achievement, or even relationships. It's putting gratitude at the center of everything you do.

Life is good.

Marshall Goldsmith
Rancho Santa Fe

Leading with Gratitude

Chapter 1

The Gratitude Gap

I t was 2008, in the midst of the global financial crisis, and WD-40 Company chief executive Garry Ridge was beginning to worry he might be coming down with something serious. "As I toured our system, people kept asking me, 'Garry, how are you?' I mean over and over. I was in my hotel room one night and lay there thinking: 'Is there a rumor I'm not well?'"

Then an aha moment struck the Australian-born executive. "It dawned on me: They weren't asking how I was; they were asking how *we* were. They wanted confirmation that our company was okay."

Like in most workplaces at the time, fear was beginning to consume employees. Ridge told us, "I decided, let's not waste a good crisis. Everywhere else our people would go they'd hear about the horror; when they came to work with us, they were going to hear about hope."

That would be a difficult task given the state of the economy, but Ridge greased the skids by communicating with his people daily. He put in place a policy of "No lying, no faking, no hiding conversations." This would be one company, he said, that would not lay off a single person or give up a single benefit, and would actually up the investment in employee learning and development during the downturn.

What's more, Ridge instructed his managers on how to lead with gratitude by showing them the benefits of regularly expressing sincere appreciation to their "tribe."

Once Ridge made it known that leading with gratitude was something he valued and expected, his leadership stepped up their own efforts by seizing the day to acknowledge and appreciate employees for living the core values. A manager might publicly thank Mark for "owning it" by helping a client understand the myriad uses of a new product. Another might commend Lisa for aiding a teammate through a challenge, embracing the value of "succeeding as a tribe." Managers began thinking of creative ways to help employees understand how they were contributing. The supply chain leader crafted a presentation that highlighted the vital ways his people were helping "sustain the company economy," another value. Leaders were not only guided to pay attention to performances that exceeded expectations but also to look for the most fundamental contributions.

The result: In 2010, the company reported its best financials in its fifty-seven-year history. And the success has kept rolling. Over the next decade, the company's market cap has grown nearly 300 percent, and they have delivered a compounded annual growth rate of total shareholder return of

15 percent (all of which equates to millions fewer squeaky door hinges and an equal number of happy teenagers successfully sneaking back in after curfew!). Employee engagement is also off the charts, with 99 percent of tribe members saying they love to work there.

All that puts WD-40 Company in an elite group of organizations.

Says Ridge, "Gratitude creates feelings of belonging. You and I have left an organization, even a relationship, because we didn't feel like we belonged. If our people know we are grateful, we are going to create an organization where they really want to come and give their best."

WHAT LEADERS AT this company discovered is the expression of gratitude for employees' efforts—when the acknowledgment is authentic, specific, and timely—can be a huge motivation and productivity booster, especially during tough times. And yet while practicing gratitude is easy, it is one of the most misunderstood and misapplied tools of management. That's a shame, because it is also one of the single most critical skills for managers to master if they want to enhance their team's performance and develop their leadership credibility.

We have devoted decades to teaching executives around the world how to be more effective, and helping them learn the art of gratitude has been central. We typically are not brought in to work with bosses who have, shall we say, a shortcoming when it comes to the social graces. No, most of these folks are thoughtful and are trying to be good leaders. In our studies, we've also observed thousands of managers in action and then talked with them about their views on leadership and how they're trying to guide and motivate their people. We've found few bosses are intentionally bullying or negligent when it comes to their people. Most also know that showing gratitude to their folks is championed as an essential part of good management. And yet again and again when we talk to their teams, we hear employees say they feel unappreciated. Some of them claim they actually feel under assault. What's the deal?

Our research and that of others shows that there is a staggering gratitude deficit in the work world. In fact, a recent study found "people are less likely to express gratitude at work than anyplace else." Meanwhile, 81 percent of working adults say they would work harder if their boss were more grateful for their work, and a whopping 96 percent of men and 94 percent of women acknowledge that a boss who expresses gratitude is more likely to be successful.

Why is there a chasm between knowing that gratitude works and the failure of so many leaders to actually practice it . . . or to do so well?

We call this the gratitude gap, and we decided to delve into what's behind it. Why in the world—we wanted to know—after so much has been written on the importance of appreciating employees over the years are there still so few leaders consistently doing it?

It's even true for star performers, whom you'd think we'd

all make more of an effort to show our gratitude to. Take this case, which may be the most glaring example of failing to show gratitude in the history of management.

An Ingratitude Slam Dunk

In 1998, Jerry Krause, then general manager of the Chicago Bulls of the National Basketball Association, uttered what has become one of the most famous quotes in sports history. "Players and coaches don't win championships," he said, "organizations do." Now, to be fair, Krause did have reason to strut and preen. His *organization* had just hauled in its sixth NBA championship in eight years (which is a ring for each finger and thumb if you're Count Rugen in *The Princess Bride*). As for Krause, he was credited as architect of the dynasty. But taking the court every night for his organization was arguably the best player ever to lace up high-tops, Michael Jordan. Alongside him was perhaps the second-best player of the nineties, Scottie Pippen, who was busting his butt—night-in, night-out—in the shadow of His Airness. Not to mention the team had a genius of a coach in Phil Jackson.

In response to Krause's statement, Jordan remarked, "What in the heck is Jerry talking about? He ain't sweating out there like I am. . . . I didn't see 'organizations' playing with the flu in Utah," a reference to his performance in game 5 of the previous year's NBA Finals, scoring 38 points against the Jazz despite severe flulike symptoms.

Jordan retired that year, while Jackson left for other op-portunities, and more than two decades later the Chicago Bulls have not won another NBA Championship.

We recount the story not only because it's an ingratitude slam dunk (sorry), but because it highlights something that might come off as a bit harsh: A lack of gratitude is a form of stupidity. It leaves on the table an enormously powerful tool not only to inspire people to reach their potential, but to actually better understand the true nature of their con-tributions.

"Leaders who treat their roles as transactional are easy to spot," Henry Timms told us. Timms is president and CEO of Lincoln Center, home to the Metropolitan Opera, New York Philharmonic, and New York City Ballet. "We've all known leaders who don't truly value their people. There's such a contrast to those who do."

Timms argues that we need a societal mind-shift on gratitude. "Many of us think about a 'debt of gratitude'—appreciating that someone's achieved something nice. We must reverse that dynamic and understand that gratitude actually inspires actions rather than responds to them."

But gratitude is not just a matter of showering more "thank-yous" and "we think you're greats" on employees. Hardly. It is not a rote checklist item or perfunctorily high-fiving team members. For expressions of gratitude to work their magic, they must be genuine and specific. Leading in this way is not only about giving credit where it's due, it's about actually *knowing* where it is due.

Developing genuine gratitude involves carefully observing what employees are doing, walking in their shoes, developing greater empathy, and sincerely trying to understand the challenges they face. It is about seeing good things happening and then expressing heartfelt appreciation for the right behaviors. On the flip side, managers who lack gratitude suffer, first and foremost, from a problem of cognition—a failure to perceive how hard their people are trying to do good work—and, if they're encountering problems, what they are. These ungrateful leaders suffer from information deficit. When we ask them why they aren't getting better results, they generally have a hard time answering.

The payoffs of getting this right come not only in boosting performance and morale, but in gaining a better understanding of your people, how they are contributing, and, frankly, what more they may have to give. The leaders who have freed themselves from their ingratitude habits have built tremendously positive and productive team cultures by actively looking for the things their people are achieving that further the values and goals of the organization. They also identify obstacles that thwart performance and are able to reinforce the right behaviors and fine-tune through positive direction.

Why Some People Say "No Thanks" to Gratitude

We cannot underestimate the morale boosting power of gratitude. A two hundred thousand–person study conducted for us by a research partner found more grateful managers lead teams with higher overall business metrics including up to two times greater profitability than their peers, an average 20 percent higher customer satisfaction, and significantly higher scores in employee engagement, including vital metrics such as trust and accountability. We've also found that when gratitude is regularly shown to employees, they feel more positive about their on-the-job contributions, are less stressed, and overall have a better sense of well-being. Wouldn't you? In addition, receiving gratitude tends to lead people to be more aware of and helpful to their colleagues and builds reciprocal appreciation for the hard work their managers are doing and the challenges they're facing.

We sat down for a few hours with Alan Mulally, the man who saved Ford Motor Company. The retired CEO said that leadership "is about people. You either understand that on a really fundamental level, or you don't. And if you do, then you love them up. You tell them everything that's going on; that's all-time respect that you create an environment where people know what the plan is, what the status is, and areas that need special attention. Then it's all about appreciating them, respecting them, and thanking them at every step of the way."

Just days after his retirement as chairman and CEO of American Express, we had a chance to interview Ken Chenault. In seventeen years in that company's top job, he created a culture focused on employee engagement and appreciation for work well done—and the results for stockholders, customers, and employees speak for themselves. He explained, "I think one of the things people get confused about is they see gratitude as simply being nice. This view of 'I want to be very stingy with gratitude' gets confused to mean I'm not being demanding. In fact, it's quite the opposite. You can be very demanding and bestow gratitude very often and be authentic."

Another urgent problem for most companies we work with is retention. An estimated $11 billion is lost in the United States alone every year due to higher-than-necessary turnover. Why do most employees leave? According to data from the U.S. Department of Labor, the number one reason people give on third-party exit interviews (those not conducted by their own organizations) is they "don't feel appreciated" by their manager for their specific contributions. It's no shock, then, to learn that our research shows frequent, genuine gratitude at work has been correlated with up to 50 percent lower employee turnover.

A leader who gets that is Jonathan Klein, chairman of Getty Images. He takes particular care to ensure his cadre of photographers feel acknowledged, as they often must risk life and limb to show the public what's happening around the world. "I have made a special effort to get to know these unsung heroes, and to thank them," he told us. "The war for talent is tough, and having the right people is the key to success. Showing gratitude goes a long way to helping great people want to stay with your company, and the appreciation leads to greater commitment."

The bottom line: There are very few high-performance leaders we've studied—who maintained outstanding results year over year—whose teams didn't have higher than average ratings in recognition/appreciation/gratitude. Being valued in this way is especially important when engaging millennial and Gen Z employees, many of whom are more accustomed to receiving extrinsic rewards than previous generations. Indeed, our Motivators Assessment, built by a team of psychologists and now taken by more than 75,000 people, has shown that the desire for expressions of gratitude at work is three times higher in people in their twenties than it is for those in their sixties.

And, if the performance results aren't compelling enough, studies have shown that expressing gratitude also brings a lift to our psyches and even our health. Scientists have found that being grateful is a bulwark against depression, boosts satisfaction with life overall, and even leads to better sleep. Those kinds of results are why gratitude has become so important to the positive psychology movement. Consider a study conducted by professors at Kent State University, who asked subjects to pen and then send a letter to someone they were grateful to. Happiness levels and life satisfaction were dramatically increased right after, and the residual effect lasted weeks. In the pursuit of happiness, gratitude has been shown to have a direct and lasting impact on the giver—thus, the more gratitude we experience and the more we offer to others, the more satisfied we generally will be with our lives. Not bad, that.

"The best way to warm your heart is to warm the heart of somebody else," says Eric Schurenberg, CEO of Mansueto Ventures, publisher of *Fast Company* and *Inc.* magazines. Which then brings us back to the core question: What holds so many people back, especially bosses, from doing just that—expressing gratitude at work?

The Negativity Bias

Adds Schurenberg, "Especially when you are a novice manager, you are so insecure that you feel like sharing credit would diminish the credit you can take. Getting over that insecurity, the impostor syndrome, is vital for a leader."

Busyness mixed with carelessness is a culprit of ingratitude, Dorie Clark told us. Clark teaches business at Duke University and is a bestselling leadership author. "There is a hesitation for some because showing gratitude means they have to admit they received help, and that erodes the myth of the self-made man or woman. It can be existentially upsetting to some who have a need for control and mastery to be forced to reckon with the fact that they needed support."

Hubert Joly, who led Best Buy through a remarkable transformation as chairman and CEO, told us, "The danger for any leader is the seduction of power, fame, glory, or money. A quirk of many successful people is they like to show they are the smartest person in the room. They are often happy to take all the help they can get without giving credit to others."

Another part of the ingratitude explanation lies in fundamental human nature. Research in psychology has shown we have a built-in tendency to give more attention to problems and perceived threats than positive things happening around us (which is why we've all probably wasted an entire day at Disneyland wondering if we locked the car!). That is dubbed the negativity bias. During early human life when our natures evolved, people had to be ever-vigilant to a host of dangers. If we missed some good news (e.g., "Grok want us come see wheel he make"), well, that was inconvenient; if we missed a piece of *bad* news ("Grok say big fire rock in sky falling here!"), that could mean the end of our lives. Thus, our brains evolved to constantly scan for bad stuff. Our workplaces today may not be stalked by saber-toothed tigers and hyenas the size of polar bears (which, seriously, recent research has shown preyed on our ancient ancestors), but they do present plenty of their own perils. In every organization we've visited, sources of stress abound: Competitors are nipping at heels, margins are tight, new products are about to be launched (late!), regulators are breathing down their necks, the CEO is new, and so on.

How can managers afford not to spend more time on the lookout for and attending to problems than looking for opportunities to be grateful? It's a survival thing.

Fair enough. But this is not a zero-sum issue. Scanning the tundra, if you will, for potential predatorial problems and devoting considerable time to preempting and/or solving them in no way precludes a leader from paying sufficient attention to the contributions of one's team. On the contrary, in times of challenge, keeping people motivated and optimistic is more vital than ever.

By withholding our gratitude in tough times, we end up shooting ourselves in the foot, said Mark Tercek, president and CEO of The Nature Conservancy. Tercek is no stranger to high-stress environments, having spent twenty-four years as a partner and managing director with investment management firm Goldman Sachs before taking the helm at this nonprofit. He told us that even well-intentioned leaders can become self-absorbed when things get challenging.

"At stressful times, I'm sometimes not conscientious enough to be mindful of all the many, many people who are helping me. So, I'm basically being a jerk," he confessed. "We need to jolt ourselves out of our self-centeredness. When I am more mindful, more aware, more thankful, our teams are happier and everybody's more engaged, focused, and productive. The same works as a parent or spouse—everybody's happier at home. It just takes discipline to slow down, be more present and aware of others, more grateful."

Some leaders think it is necessary to withhold positive sentiments at times in order to keep pressure on team members. "If we keep them on edge, they'll work harder" is the thinking. That mentality is about as valid as a Blockbuster Video free-rental coupon. Pressure like that increases anxiety, and anxiety undermines productivity. In comparison, research from Robert Emmons of the University of California, Davis, shows that a leader who is more grateful amid difficult circumstances can help people cope. "In the face of demoralization," he explains, "gratitude has the power to energize. In the face of brokenness, gratitude has the power to heal. In the face of despair, gratitude has the power to bring hope."

A great irony of the negativity bias is that it leads us to lose sight of another ingrained aspect of human nature: the ethic of reciprocity. While scientists are only starting to pinpoint the exact biological nature of gratitude, more than two centuries ago economist and philosopher Adam Smith conjectured that gratitude evolved in humans as we began to group together in communities. Society, he argued, only works if we repay the help we get from those around us. If we don't reciprocate assistance given with appreciation, we end up provoking intense resentment. In the social sphere, we would be cut off from the group. At work, we can't just shun our bosses, but we can most surely resent them. In a Florida State University study, one of the top reasons employees gave for resenting their managers was that they "failed to give credit where credit was due."

THE REALITY IS, no amount of adversity should prevent a leader from seeing value that's being created and expressing gratitude for it. While many think that the time for expressing thanks is when all problems are solved, progressive leaders know otherwise. Indeed, we have seen firsthand that even in the direst of circumstances, people's lives are enormously enriched when they are grateful. Let us tell you one special story that illustrates the point.

We were profoundly moved by a conversation we had with Rebecca Douglas, who founded a charity called Rising Star Outreach. Her foundation's goal is to help the one thousand leprosy colonies in India thrive and become self-sufficient. Rising Star works with the poorest people on earth, the so-called untouchables.

Douglas met two brothers, David and Daniel, in India about a decade ago. After one of them—Daniel—had been diagnosed and treated for leprosy, these stick-thin boys fled the leprosy colony where they had lived with only the clothes on their backs, seeking an escape from unimaginable poverty and misery. A young mother in Arizona, Lynn Allred, saw a picture of the boys at a talk Douglas was giving and wanted to help. Allred worked tirelessly for two years to find a way to bring David and Daniel to America to study and finally found a private school willing to accept them, even though they were years behind in their studies and didn't speak English.

Rebecca Douglas traveled to India to tell the boys about this remarkable opportunity. She interviewed them to capture their thoughts for the school's admission essay. After all the questions were answered, she asked if there was anything else the boys would like to say. Daniel paused only for a moment and said, "Please add that of all the boys in the world, I am the most blessed."

"This malnourished boy who owned only the clothes on his back," she told us, "and had been afflicted with one of the most dreaded diseases in the world; who had been forced to work in the hot sun as an unpaid laborer instead of attending school; who had endured all kinds of unspeakable privation—still had his heart overflowing with gratitude."

Since then, says Douglas, when she finds herself tempted to whine from whatever challenges or overwhelm she might be experiencing, she remembers the boy filled with gratitude who taught her to be thankful in all circumstances.

As it turned out, David and Daniel had more reasons to be grateful. Against all odds, they were sponsored by the Allreds and came to America to study. Today David is an MBA student, while Daniel returned to India—with a coveted American college degree in hand—to help his people.

Douglas left us with sage words: "Gratitude attracts more gratitude. It has nothing to do with your circumstances and everything to do with your heart."

Of Skeptics and Believers

We know there is no lack of cynicism about the benefits of gratitude in the business world, and some of it may even come from a real place. The skeptics often recall a time in their childhoods—perhaps following a birthday—when Mom or Dad sat them down and under threat of grounding forced them to write out thank-you notes to Grandma and Aunt Gertie. Or maybe at work HR instituted a program for them to be more appreciative to their peers, but in a culture of low trust it was met with only halfhearted adoption and cringe-worthy comments from the skeptics. While for some, efforts encouraging gratitude would be taken as a prompt to take action, for others, the formalized, prescribed way stuck in the craw.

Former NFL quarterback turned entrepreneur Chad Pennington told us some skepticism comes when employees see leaders using gratitude from a "self-service point of view. They have an attitude of: 'If I express this gratitude to you, then I expect this back.' Those leaders are going down the wrong path," he said.

Pennington said that gratitude is in fact the highest form of servant leadership. "People with humility don't think less of themselves; they think about themselves less. It's a true sign of strength to suppress your own pride and ego, something all of us have, and put somebody else in front of us."

So, no matter your past experiences, we intend to convince you that gratitude is not only good for your people and your business—it's good for you. And we are going teach you how to get past any reservations you may be harboring and embrace gratitude effectively.

The leaders we've interviewed certainly are believers. These women and men are tremendously busy, with many of them running billion-dollar enterprises. As neurotic George Costanza says in *Seinfeld*, "They are men with jobs, Jerry! They wear suits and ties. They are married, they have secretaries." Yet they found time to talk about how gratitude has helped them transform their businesses and their lives. To a person, they wanted us to let other leaders—(i.e., you)—know how essential it is to be grateful to those in our care.

Gail Miller is one of the best of them. A decade ago—after her husband, Larry, died—she assumed full ownership and the chairman's post of a multibillion-dollar business empire that includes sixty car dealerships, a movie theater chain, finance and insurance companies, and the Utah Jazz basketball team. It was a role she questioned even wanting, but with ten thousand jobs at stake, she realized she didn't have much choice.

"I had been a stay-at-home mom most of my married life," Miller told us. "When Larry was building the company, I was afraid I was being left behind. I didn't have an education; I was dealing with kids all day. I felt awkward when I went out with him to business functions where he was meeting high-profile people. I had to find a way to develop myself."

Miller visited a counselor who taught her to consider the unique perspective she brought to the world. She realized she had a voice, and the way to share it was to say affirmative things. "To do that I had to pay more attention to what was happening around me, to be grateful for everything that impacts my life. That makes it easy to say, 'I see how hard you worked on that.' People are dying for that."

For Miller, who has since grown and expanded her business empire and her family's significant philanthropic efforts, gratitude has "unlocked the fullness of life and created a vision for tomorrow."

As to those who still don't believe, we have found that the bias to the negative is not solely to blame. While probing the views of a host of managers in organizations around the world about this practice, we discovered a set of widely held beliefs about managing people that cause many to withhold their gratitude. We call these pernicious beliefs the Ingratitude Myths, and they are holding people back from achieving all they can. In the next part of this book, we are going to attempt to debunk them once and for all. We encourage you to read through each, even if you think some might not apply to you. Chances are you'll see leaders you know in all of them, and yourself in at least a few. If you don't, you are truly unique.

After the myths, we'll roll up our sleeves and get to work in Part II by introducing eight simple ways to do an expert job of showing employees they are valued. We'll include stories of how some of today's most successful leaders—such as CEOs Alan Mulally of Ford and Hubert Joly of Best Buy—incorporated gratitude into their incredibly successful leadership styles. We are confident their ideas and examples will make it irrefutably clear that showing gratitude isn't just about being nice, it's about being smart—really smart—and is a skill that everyone can easily learn.

As you work through these how-tos, you will learn to shift your focus to expressing appreciation for *who* people are, not just their actions.

As the title of this book suggests, *Leading with Gratitude* was written to help managers striving to engage and inspire their teams. But it is just as much for the increasing number of employees who feel devalued and forgotten. It is our hope that embracing these ideas will reignite passion and drive in everyone.

We believe there is a more positive, hopeful future out there for us all. No matter where you are starting from, no matter the challenges you face, as you apply these concepts, you will begin to benefit from the transformative power of gratitude.

Part I

The Ingratitude Myths
(That Are Holding Leaders Back)

Chapter 2

Myth: Fear Is the Best Motivator

Let's face it: ABSOLUTELY NO ONE thinks they lead with fear. Yet there are fear-based managers everywhere, and no one dares tell them the truth.

Part of the problem is that word *fear*. It conjures up images of a boss from a bygone era—straight out of central casting—growling threats as he puffs stale smoke clouds from his stogie. What manager today would intentionally keep their people in a constant state of anxiety? Are we right?

Actually, in our surveys, we found about a third of managers subscribe to the notion of using fear in some ways, and most are unaware they are doing it.

Fear at work is manifest in a myriad of ways. For example, a manager who lacks confidence can spread fear around a workplace as fast as a funky cologne. He might be intimidated by employees who shine and feel it's necessary to put them in their place, or he may utter such motivating words as "If we don't hit our goals next month, I don't know if I can protect you guys." Or "There's a long list of people who'd love your jobs." His employees can then spend their afternoons realizing how lucky they are. Or not.

Another example? While many managers do not consciously try to fan fear's flames, they aren't exactly trying to stamp them out either. Hey, if their people feel a little extra pressure, then is it really their responsibility to put it to rest? *They just have to toughen up. Fear comes along with the paycheck. Whatever doesn't kill you makes you stronger.* And so on.

The fact is, we all know instinctively that fear can get stuff done. If anxiety levels amp up sufficiently, people can do some pretty crazy things for short periods of time. We've all heard the story of the mom who lifts a Pontiac off a trapped family member. Marketers have long known the power of fear, using it to sell everything from life insurance to alarm systems to mouthwash to fiber cereals that taste like tree bark and feet.

It's also true that a degree of anxiety in the workplace is simply unavoidable, especially with all the disruptions we face today. Upstart competitors are introducing new technologies that may indeed threaten job security. When it comes to preparing an important assignment, a quiver of anxiety is generally accepted as a sign you want to step up your efforts. As for employees who are not performing well, if they're conscientious and able to evaluate their work objectively, intrinsic fear can lead to improved results. That's the fear-of-failure argument.

All of this depends on one thing: that fear doesn't tie people up in knots. Which is too often the case.

Edwards Deming, for one, concluded that fear was anathema in a culture of Total Quality Management. "Drive out fear, so that everyone may work effectively," he wrote. As Deming keenly understood, the effects of fear are generally corrosive of performance over time. His insight is backed up by voluminous recent research, such as a survey by Glassdoor that found while 81 percent of people say they're motivated to work harder when their boss shows appreciation for their work, by contrast only 38 percent report working harder when their boss is demanding, and just 37 percent say they work harder if they fear losing their job.

When it comes to our daily work and broader life challenges, fear is most definitely not the best motivator. Not even close. It causes a host of ill effects that undermine the quality of people's work and overall team performance. That's because at the heart of fear is doubt, and in doubt-filled cultures—with people wondering, *Will I be in trouble, get yelled at, be fired?*—the constant uncertainty kills motivation, not to mention innovation.

Cultures like that provoke prolonged stress, which is our built-in biological reaction to fear. When faced with a threat—real or imagined—the brain's amygdala sends out a distress signal, prompting the release of stress hormones, which cause a number of physiological changes, such as increased heartbeat, quickened breathing, and muscle tensing. This reaction is designed as a boon in response to immediate threats, giving us a surge of energy and enhancing our strength. *Shazam!* But all that was intended as a *temporary* response to danger, not as a prolonged state of being. Continuously perceived threats, ones that stretch out day-to-day and week-to-week, sap energy. Chronic stress can also seriously undermine the quality of people's sleep, further undercutting their energy. Fear-induced stress is a major factor in burnout.

Another reaction to fear is the fight-or-flight response, to which should be added the "deer caught in the headlights" non-reaction. When it comes to our work, a persistent sense of threat leads to versions of these responses that come with a host of productivity-crushing effects. Getting people into fight mode might sound terrific for some leaders—"Good! They'll be charged up to tackle the challenge!" But a fighting spirit, when evoked by fear rather than inspiration and a sense of purpose, is too often aimed right back against the manager who provoked it instead of the challenges to be tackled.

Leaders should never underestimate the degree of bald-faced contempt that people let brew in response to what they perceive as unfair and harsh treatment, or even the perception that a manager isn't really trying to solve the problems that are causing them to freak out in the first place. Leaders often don't even realize they are creating this kind of stress. One such manager we were asked to coach told us she considered herself "demanding" but "fair." In preparation for coaching this woman to improve her people skills, we conducted a 360 and interviewed her team and some colleagues around the organization. Comments included "Tries to keep us off-balance," and "Blames everything on the SLT (senior leadership team)," and the unforgettable: "Wants sheep-like compliance but has no idea where we are heading."

With leaders like her, employees often try to undermine their manager's authority, sometimes not even caring about what the long-term consequences might be for their own careers. This kind of "screw you" subterfuge can actually be hard to detect—especially given how busy leaders are. Disgruntled team members can spend hours a day rallying their colleagues against their manager, building solidarity by venting war stories. "Do you know what he said to me this morning?!" or "I can't believe how she treated you in that meeting!" As to speaking up about problems, fugetaboutit. We hear sentiments such as "He's doing nothing to help me; why should I help him?"

The problem is, when people work in fear-based cultures, they tend to defend themselves—spending a good deal of time, and psychic energy, on finding reasons they're not the ones at fault. They may blame management or other departments for the crappy products they have to sell, the rigid processes they have to follow, or the IT system that goes down without warning. In their teams, they spend their days looking for colleagues to pin blame on rather than accepting even a modicum of accountability themselves.

In short, Machiavelli's famous axiom "It's better to be feared than loved" is not only wrong but dangerous.

Are You Managing with Fear by Mistake?

When we have to tell a leader he or she is instilling a degree of fear in their team, as you can imagine, it often does not go well. It's usually met with surprise and resistance. "Whaddayamean I *scare* my people?!" As we have to explain, explicit threats are far from the only way of instilling fear. Sometimes it is fanned when a leader focuses on finding fault more than praising success. When managers hint that jobs are at stake, for example, they sometimes think they're doing employees a favor by giving them a subtle heads-up. Other leaders fall into the trap of looking for someone to blame each time there's a problem, focusing more on the negative than on rallying the team to correct and learn from missteps. One common mistake is expressing irritation when people ask for guidance. Another massive problem is micromanaging, which implies the leader has little faith in a person's ability and is on a constant hunt for mistakes to criticize. And, in reality, it is often a manifestation of the leader's own fear of failure.

Ken Chenault, retired chairman and CEO of American Express, told us, "Some people want to present this image of being very tough—they confuse being decisive with being compassionate. One of the fundamental beliefs they miss is this: If you want to be an effective leader, you have to capture the hearts and minds of people. Part of gratitude is being vulnerable, but some leaders are very cautious about showing any vulnerability." He added that these types of leaders do not establish the level of personal connection necessary to be meaningful in other people's lives.

To get a read on whether fear may be holding back the performance of your team, consider this set of common symptoms we've observed in fear-based cultures:

- Outbursts are allowed, especially if from a senior leader
- Inappropriate conduct is tolerated, especially if from a top performer
- Communication is one-way (down), and employees would not feel comfortable challenging the boss
- Core values are not clearly articulated, understood, and certainly not followed
- When someone is called into the boss's office, the first thought is, "Am I in trouble?"
- Meetings before meetings allow employees to spin things in the way leaders will want to hear them

As for those who persist in instilling fear after they become aware they are doing it, consider the common justification we hear next, something along the lines of . . .

I Don't Need to Be Their Friend, I Need Their Respect

Badass managers get a lot done, they claim. They point out exemplars like Bobby Knight, former Indiana Hoosiers basketball coach, who won three NCAA championships and famously let rip on his teams with a seemingly hair-trigger temper. One executive told us, "To turn a company around, you've got to show people you have guts, you can't be afraid to be the hard-ass. I think people admire that about me." As we conducted his 360, comments from peers and employees included: "He pushes and pushes until we just reach our limit," "Micromanages," and "He overrules consensus with his own views." He didn't sound very admired to us.

Imagine for a moment this scenario. Milton and Lois are taking a quick coffee break after a morning meeting with their manager.

Milton: Ugh! I can't stand our boss.

Lois: *[nods]* The man is a blight. An embarrassment to human reproduction.

Milton: Hate. His. Guts.

Lois: But you gotta *respect* him.

Milton: Oh yeah, no doubt. Total respect for the man. Tons and tons of respect.

Lois: Oh, me, too. But I still hate him.

Milton: Can't even breathe for the hatred!

Is that ever gonna happen? Of course not. No one is named Milton or Lois anymore.

It's Not Cool to Be Kind

The Fear Myth tends to persist, consciously or subconsciously, because fearmongers get a lot of attention in our society. With the bombastic, nasty behavior of many successful people on public display, it can appear the fastest way to get ahead is to be cutting and cruel, to make sarcastic comments to show off with, or to insinuate a greater level of intelligence or dominance over others. This has created a more divisive, cynical, and arrogant world in which it can be increasingly difficult for people to admit their vulnerabilities, to show themselves as being anything less than perfect because others are on the lookout for missteps (even if they happened decades ago).

We love what Scott O'Neil told us about this so-called bravado. He's CEO of Harris Blitzer Sports & Entertainment, a multibillion-dollar portfolio company that includes the New Jersey Devils and Philadelphia 76ers. "Being edgy is cheap intellectualism," he said.

We could not agree more.

No, what we find is that cultivating respect is more about love than fear. So says Jake Wood.

After playing offensive line for the University of Wisconsin football team, Wood served a tour of duty in the Marine Corps in Iraq and then as a scout-sniper in Afghanistan. He's now the cofounder of Team Rubicon, a charity that couples military veterans with first responders to deploy as emergency response teams when disasters strike around the world. This tough guy argues that authentically caring about those in our charge creates that sought-after respect. As he puts it, "No one will risk their life for you if they don't feel loved."

Just two weeks into his first tour in Iraq, Wood's sergeant was seriously injured after their convoy hit a roadside bomb. As a young corporal, Wood was left in charge of a team of marines whom he had to wake each day and convince to head back into the Triangle of Death, the most deadly zone of fighting in the country at the time. Wood said, "You have to know who your people are and where they want to go in life. They knew I loved them and cared for them. And if one of them went down, we would all run through machine gun fire to bring him home."

This lesson somehow had eluded another former military man in a training session. The retired general, who now works in the corporate world, was particularly struck when the discussion came around to how fear-based leaders believe they would undermine their own authority by going soft and showing gratitude. He admitted he had fallen into this trap in his soldiering days, and it had trickled into his home life. With tears welling, this tough-as-nails man committed to change and added, "Maybe then my children will talk to me."

The fact is, people aren't going to give their all unless their leaders drop fear-based tactics and display caring behaviors: being transparent and fair, listening, admitting their own mistakes, and acting in the team's best interests. Developing respect is about helping others grow and supporting people who make honest mistakes. It includes sharing the credit and absorbing blame when needed. It means living up to the team's cornerstone values and insisting on ethical behavior from teammates. Respect is about providing compassionate and honest feedback and having tough conversations.

When those behaviors are in place, fear is the last thing on anyone's mind. The good news is that it's almost never too late to change a culture of fear.

Simple Practices Can Work Wonders

When Alan Mulally became CEO at Ford, an unhealthy degree of fear had infected the leadership ranks of the venerable American motor company. Executive meetings, for instance, had become places of combat in which employees tried to identify flaws in each other's plans instead of recommending solutions.

Mulally told us, "The businesses were all separate around the world; there was very little working together." He assembled all the sixteen top leaders from around the world every Thursday for a business plan review, intending to bring them together on the vision, strategy, and plan. "This was all new and, of course, they were apprehensive. But it sounded good to them. It sounded like, 'My gosh, we're going to move into the light.'"

A goal for Mulally was to infuse his eleven practices of a "working-together management system" he had developed as CEO of Boeing—principles from "People first . . . love them up" to "Respect, listen, help, and appreciate each other." All this, he believed, would create a Ford where people could have open and honest discussions without fear of blame and would reframe the executive team meetings from negative to positive.

"Like in most companies, Ford had operated on a philosophy that you only bring an issue to your boss or your leader if you have an answer," Mulally told us. "The new philosophy was based on the fact that we are going to have problems, and we're going to need everybody's help to solve them. So one of the expected behaviors is that we're going to share and ask for help when we need it, and then we're all going to be committed to helping."

It took a while for his direct team to believe he was sincere.

Finally, in one meeting, North American president Mark Fields took a chance and admitted a new vehicle launch under his purview would be delayed. Other executives looked on nervously. Mulally said, "The air went out of the room. I could see it in people's eyes that they thought doors would open up behind Mark and two large human beings would remove him. 'Bye-bye, Mark.'"

Instead, Mulally began a round of applause and said, "Mark, thank you so much. That is great visibility." Then he asked the group, "Is there anything we can we do to help Mark out?" Within seconds, ideas were flying around the room.

Since we weren't in the meeting, we've always pictured this moment with more drama than probably existed, with Mulally beginning a slow, deliberate golf clap over sweeping violins, which crescendo into raucous applause by all. Tears are wiped. Roll credits. In reality, said Mulally, it passed in the blink of an eye but changed everything. As he frequently told his leaders, "You *have* a problem; *you* are not the problem."

Turning around an organization means more than fixing the numbers. Yes, Mulally increased sales, profit, and cash flow and reduced debt. But often those are symptoms of a company that has gotten off course. Mulally eliminated infighting by creating transparency and a working-together culture across all his leadership teams. Doing this allowed the culture to be united with confidence, as opposed to breaking up into the fragmented groups as it had been. As evidence that it worked, employee commitment soared. When Mulally arrived at Ford, employee engagement hovered around 20 percent; when he retired eight years later, it was the highest in the world of any large company at 91 percent.

"The leader is really, really important," he said. "The world out there is now figuring this out: Skills are one thing, but to create a smart and healthy organization, void of politics, where people don't go after each other, that's about respecting them, showing them the data, and thanking them for what they've done."

In the second half of this book, we'll introduce a number of simple but powerful ways to tamp down fear and bolster confidence, enhance team solidarity, and boost energy through innovative gratitude practices.

As you'll find, when the right behaviors are in place, there is little time spent in fear. Everyone is having too much fun winning.

Chapter 3

Myth: People Want *Way* Too Much Praise These Days

We met Anne, a successful pharmaceutical sales rep, when visiting one of our clients. The head of sales told us what a coup it had been to poach her from a competitor, as they had lost business to Anne for years. In just a few minutes together it was clear that she is not only whip smart but has a wonderful sense of humor. She told us she had performed in an improv comedy troupe in college and now puts her wit to work, talking her way past medical office receptionists and into the offices of harried physicians. By the end of many of her sales calls, the doctors not only commit to her company's drug line but ask when she'll be back. That is *unheard-of* in medical sales.

When we asked her who in the world had been foolish enough to let her get away, she let out a little sigh and told us about her old manager. "He asked me one day what he could do to improve the workplace. I was really surprised because he managed with an iron fist. But I figured, well, great, maybe he really wants to change things. So I explained that I didn't feel like I got much gratitude from him for my contributions, and I said even just a little thanks now and again would be nice.

"Later that day he and I were heading out on some calls and he mocked me almost nonstop. 'Hey, nice job opening the door' . . . 'Wow, you turned the radio down perfectly!' He thought it was hilarious and told me to lighten up when he could see I wasn't amused. That was the night I started polishing my résumé."

We've met many managers who tell us employees are way too hungry for approval these days. This sentiment has flared up in recent years as millennials and Gen Zs have become the majority of the workforce, bringing with them distinctive expectations about work-life balance, a need for meaning, a penchant for Top Ramen, and a fearlessness to change jobs if they don't like what they find. Many managers we talk with complain that younger generations are immature and needy—often invoking the popular notion that helicopter parenting has made them praise-crazed. They've told us, "I don't want to feed the fire by patting their backs" or "They need to realize what the world is really like."

They worry if they give out more praise their workers will get big heads, become overconfident, and start to slack off. And worst of all, they may demand more money.

Now, it is actually true that overpraise of a certain kind— practiced by some parents—has had adverse effects on children. We'll talk about that research more in just a few pages. But first, every leader needs to understand that our research, and that of many others, shows what younger workers are really looking for is not praise for praise's sake, but guidance. Clear direction and feedback. They want to know what they're doing that's right and what they're doing that may be off course. Those who do seek praise often have high self-esteem (like Anne). For them, gratitude provides clarity about whether the work they are doing is correct, valued by the boss or others, and making a significant contribution to the business.

More than twenty-five thousand millennials and Gen Zs have now taken our Motivators Assessment, and our analysis of their answers shows what the vast majority most desire from their managers is consistent feedback on the impact they are making. Most have grown up with more coaching from their parents, teachers, and actual coaches than any prior generation. They've also never been without instantaneous access to information and people. Ever. Airdrop a millennial buck naked into the middle of the Moroccan desert and pretty soon he'll be Instagramming with four bars on an iPhone he's miraculously produced. In short, our younger workers are used to getting immediate answers to their questions. That's a vital role gratitude fills—it helps people know they are on the right track.

The good news for managers? Our work with employees of all ages makes it clear that the desire for more frequent, clear feedback is by no means a particular quirk of millennials. What's different is they have the unmitigated temerity to actually expect it, and to speak up about it. In fact, research shows there is good reason for employees, of whatever age, to be looking for more feedback. According to a survey published in *Forbes*, 65 percent of all employees would like more feedback than they currently get.

So rather than seeing younger workers as problem children making demands for praise, consider that they are offering invaluable insight into how managers can better motivate and steer all their people. We love what Kris Duggan, founder of HR software company Betterworks, says in this regard. "There is a common misconception that young employees expect to be rewarded for every single thing they do. The truth is that they prefer only to be recognized for significant accomplishments, just as any other employee would. More important, though, is for them to feel that their contributions matter for the future of the company."

Backing up Duggan is popular millennial blogger Kaytie Zimmerman. She writes, "What normal employee doesn't want to be recognized, thanked, and praised for a job well done? This is not just a millennial desire. We all have a deep-rooted need to know our work matters, regardless of our age. The difference in millennials is that they do not feel loyal to a company simply because they were hired by them. They are loyal when they feel appreciated, challenged, and rewarded."

Narcissism and the Problem with Praise

Okay, so what about the narcissism epidemic—certainly that's been fueled by praise, right? Joel Stein's data published in *Time* shows that narcissism is indeed on the rise, but he points out that narcissism isn't a new thing and is not solely the fault of young people. "The self-involvement millennials are known for is more a continuation of a trend than a revolutionary break from previous generations," he said.

Has praise played a role in that trend? Yes and no. According to one study conducted by Ohio State University and University of Amsterdam researchers, narcissism in children comes not from praise itself, but *undue* and constant approval from parents who have an overinflated view of how special their children are. "Research shows that narcissism is higher in Western countries than non-Western countries and suggests that narcissism levels have been steadily increasing among Western youth over the past few decades," the authors wrote in *Proceedings of the National Academy of Sciences*.

By definition, narcissists feel superior to others, fantasize about personal successes, and believe they deserve special treatment. When humiliated, they often lash out aggressively or even violently. In digging into the causes of narcissism, the researchers had parents and their children, ages seven to eleven, answer a set of questions such as whether they viewed themselves as exceptional. Two such statements to rate were "I am superior to others" and "I am entitled to privileges." Their parents were also asked to rate statements about the "value" of their kids, such as "My child is a great example for other children to follow." They found that the children of the parents who rated their kids highest generally showed the strongest tendency toward narcissism. What's more, those same children did not, however, have higher self-esteem. Note: Self-esteem means thinking well of oneself, whereas narcissism involves passionately *wanting* to think well of oneself.

Narcissism, the researchers suggest, is predicted most by parental overvaluation. Children internalize their parents' inflated views of them. Self-esteem, on the other hand, is predicted by parental warmth. So, stressing over and over to kids how exceptional they are in every aspect of life can cause problems with a child's ability to assess their own level of skills and talents.

The key to offering effective praise to a child is to frequently give acknowledgment to positive behaviors. We've read just about every study ever conducted on praise, and we have yet to find one credible set of findings that shows regular, *deserved* praise leads to inflated egos. On the contrary, research dating back more than seventy years has shown offering reinforcement for positive behaviors and work well done is essential in rearing healthy, well-adjusted kids.

When managers withhold legitimate praise because they think employees have had too much of it already, they're essentially taking on a parental role. Obviously that's a danger (if not a bit creepy). While leaders should mentor employees and help them develop their talents, no leader should try to take on the job of "fixing" who an employee is. This parent-child leadership relationship creates a culture in which workers wait to receive assignments, taking little ownership themselves. As for leaders, it leads to a disproportionate effort in correcting people's ways of being ("Stand up straight, Tareek, you're slouching again") rather than focusing on improving their output and potential to grow.

I Don't Give What I Didn't Get

An irony of the Too Much Myth is that it often stems from a leader having received little enough gratitude him or herself. Some of these managers have told us they received sparse praise coming up from their own bosses, and from their parents, and even today they don't get much of it from the executive they report to—yet they still kept coming in to work every day and made their way up the ranks, didn't they? "I hardly even *saw* my first boss," one of them told us, "and he sure as heck never told me I was going a good job." (There's a reason unrequited love is the main source of so much popular music: We can all relate.)

While some exceptional people have built strong characters out of what they didn't get—a lack of stability in childhood made them more thoughtful parents, the absence of mentors made them better bosses, a scarcity of good friends as a child made them more trusted confidants as adults—it's more common that those who didn't get something pass that sin of omission along to the next generation, and the people who work for leaders who maintain this myth too often become dispirited and disengaged.

Why would we pass the buck like that? At root is the

deep-seated psychology of reciprocity. This powerful innate ethic tells us that we shouldn't give what we didn't get, and vice versa. That cycle must be broken. First of all, leaders who fall into this trap need to remember it wasn't their employees who gave them short shrift, so this isn't really a situation in which reciprocity should be the arbiter. The right measure of whether or not to offer gratitude is whether or not it's due. Period. And while many of us may have hung tough and kept plugging along in our careers despite a lack of props from our own stingy bosses, that just won't wash with today's employees. This is one way in which millennials are most certainly distinct. They are not afraid to jump ship when their managers are too thrifty with their thanks.

Not long ago, Adrian was conducting a training at a Silicon Valley technology giant. After introducing research showing the most engaged employees are recognized more often than their less-engaged peers, and that this particular company's engagement survey showed its recognition scores were, ahem, sucky, one man countered with: "My first boss didn't say good job very often, but when he did you knew he meant it." Another manager spoke up: "That may have worked for you, Rod, but act like that today and your programmers will leave you."

Managers like Rod often admit that they don't feel comfortable expressing gratitude and believe others will feel uncomfortable receiving it. After all, we've all known people who seem awkward receiving compliments, who refute them by putting themselves down. "I love that outfit" is met with

"Oh, this old thing. It's getting so ratty." While it's true that some may have a hard time receiving praise, or even believing they deserve it, when appreciation is expressed about on-the-job achievements—whether they show it or not—people are typically pleased that their work is being acknowledged. Getting into the swing of things might take some practice for managers or employees who don't feel comfortable expressing or receiving it, but the human animal has been crafted to appreciate *authentic* appreciation. We can generally get into gear with it fairly quickly. The trick is to be brave and give this a shot, no matter what the critics (external or internal) say.

We love what US President Teddy Roosevelt said in 1910: "It is not the critic who counts. . . . The credit belongs to the man who is actually in the arena, whose face is marred by dust and sweat and blood; who strives valiantly; who errs, who comes short again and again, because there is no effort without error and shortcoming." University of Houston professor and author Brené Brown says she had an entirely different life before finding that quote. "You are going to fall, fail, and you're going to know heartbreak. [But] these are the words I say before my feet hit the floor every day: 'Today, I'll choose courage over comfort. . . . Today, I'm gonna choose to be brave.'" Hurrah!

There is one last possibility that is important to mention. In our work developing the Motivators Assessment, we found that a small percentage of people (more common with older workers) are much more intrinsically driven than the norm and therefore will tell you they don't want a lot of praise. A few may even interpret your gratitude as a form of condescension. "Look, I really don't need you to lavish praise on me," they may say. It's easy then to assume that gratitude is not important to them at all. But in reality, in most cases that's not true. For strongly intrinsically driven individuals, praise needs to be brief and absolutely on target. Remember that it is a rarefied thing indeed for people not to want any positive, direct feedback from their manager. When Jim Kouzes and Barry Posner, authors of *The Leadership Challenge*, have asked survey respondents, "When you get encouragement, does it help you perform at a higher level?" some 98 percent of people say yes. So, it's a good assumption that everyone wants some gratitude. The trick is doing it in the way they value.

When Is There Too Much of a Good Thing?

It's rare when praise of the targeted and authentic type is too much, though clearly some gratitude can be overdone. Some rain is good, too much is a flood, right? After visiting hundreds of workplaces all around the world, however, we've yet to encounter a place where employees have complained about being overpraised. "I am outta here! Phyllis, pack my things! These SOBs have gone too far with all these plaques and balloons!" Hardly. What's more typical is that workers feel their efforts are largely overlooked.

Still, some managers argue that if they give people positive feedback all the time, the blush will go off the rose. A fascinating study conducted at the Wharton School at the University of Pennsylvania showed results about the frequency of appreciation that might be quite surprising. The researchers randomly divided university fundraisers into two groups, one of which made phone calls to solicit alumni donations in the same way they always had, while the second group received daily verbal expressions of gratitude from the director of annual giving. The employees who received those frequent and specific words of gratitude made 50 percent more fundraising calls than those who did not. Targeted praise didn't get old for these Ivy League school employees. In fact, it helped keep them motivated in a challenging job day after day.

Now, we aren't saying that every manager needs to offer praise to every employee every day. What we are saying is that most managers should be offering more of it, quite a bit more often.

We've found the research by psychologists John Gottman and Robert Levenson particularly illuminating. They began doing longitudinal studies of married couples in the 1970s to understand the difference between happy and unhappy pairings. In one line of their research, they invited couples into a room with video equipment—which the couples were aware of—and asked the pairs to take about fifteen minutes to try to solve a conflict in their relationship. It could be anything from finances to in-laws to kids to which way the toilet paper should hang, or whatever was giving them grief at the time.

The researchers then analyzed the tapes, detailing the nature of the couple's interactions. Then they put the tapes away—rewinding them, naturally, since these were very considerate researchers. (Note: That joke was only for people older than thirty.)

Nine years later, they checked in with the couples to find out whether they were still married. What they discovered was that in those brief attempts at conflict resolution all those years earlier, the couples who had stayed together showed a distinct ratio of positive to negative statements: It was five positives to each negative. For those who had divorced, the ratio of positive to negative was less than one to one. Going forward, using this fifteen-minute interaction alone, the researchers were able to predict with more than 90 percent accuracy whether couples would stay together. Wow.

Dr. Gottman said of the happiest couples, "They may be arguing, but they are also laughing and teasing and there are signs of affection because they have emotional connections. On the other hand, unhappy couples tend to engage in fewer positive interactions to compensate for their escalating negativity. If the positive-to-negative ratio during conflict is one-to-one or less, that's unhealthy, and it indicates a couple teetering on the edge of divorce." Thanks in part to this research, therapists now have partners demonstrate gratitude to each other as an important component of couples' therapy.

In the next part of the book, we'll offer more specific guidance on how to gauge whether or not you're providing a healthy quotient of gratitude to your people. For now, we'll leave you with this: Our research backs up Gottman and Levenson's findings. At work as in our personal relationships, a five-to-one ratio of positive to interactions to constructive criticism is a good indicator of a high-performance culture.

Chapter 4

Myth: There's Just No Time

The one thing all leaders lack in their twelve-hour days is time. We have yet to meet a manager who isn't crazy busy with back-to-back meetings, e-mails stacking up, and fires to put out. Busyness is by far the most common excuse for not expressing gratitude.

We are sympathetic; we know what it's like. We've served in VP roles in several large corporations and today, as entrepreneurs, run a training company, write books, speak to organizations, and do executive coaching and culture consulting. Last year we worked in more than eighty cities on five continents. But practicing gratitude well doesn't take that much time, and the returns in productivity far outweigh those of any other management practice.

Most leaders we've met who subscribe to the Time Myth believe gratitude is nice and all, but their effectiveness is about the hard stuff, not the soft stuff. With the speed of business today, the onslaught of data to be analyzed, and competitive pressures more intense than ever, management is about finding insights and ahas. It's about developing knowledge of the competitive landscape and reporting up what they find. It's about fixing, not thanking. When it comes to face-to-face time, meetings with customers and suppliers and developing relationships with peers and superiors around the organization are often seen as more important than time with one's team. Not that they don't spend time with their team members, they argue, but there's only so much time in the day and they just can't do more.

Of course, data, customers, peers in leadership positions, and the like are all crucial, time-intensive priorities. But at the same time, competitive pressures make effective people management more critical than ever. Workers leave for competitors more readily today, and turnover is one of the greatest expenses and productivity killers of our day. Conservatively, Deloitte estimates the cost of losing each employee ranges from tens of thousands of dollars to one and a half to two times the employee's annual salary. Costs include ramp-up time to reach peak productivity, hiring, onboarding, training, loss of engagement from colleagues due to high turnover, and increased mistakes and errors.

And who is most likely to leave you high and dry? It's certainly not your slackers. They aren't going anywhere. Literally. You could park the team coffeepot on their desk and they wouldn't quit. The most proficient and highly motivated employees are those most likely to be scanning for possibilities and are prime targets for poachers. Consider for just a moment the effect on your team's productivity—and likely your own job—over the next quarter, and even full year, if your highest-performing person or two jumped ship.

When we reflect on the Time Myth, we can't help but think of one prospective client. We had an exploratory meeting with this man, the chair of a large manufacturer who had heard we'd done a lot of research on building high-performance cultures. That, he said, was exactly what he wanted. As we broached the topic of soft skills and how managers and employees in the highest-performing teams expressed more gratitude to each other, he stopped the conversation cold. His managers could practice that kind of stuff when they were "at church," he said. While his people were on the job, they needed to focus on building the business.

In the end, he decided not to amp up his culture's focus on soft skills, and over the next few years he oversaw declining sales, innovation, and a 60 percent reduction in stock price at his firm. Of course, we aren't suggesting a lack of gratitude was the sole reason his organization tanked (we think they also removed the Ping-Pong table). But a review of more than three hundred of the most recent Indeed and Glassdoor reviews of the company told us a culture of gratitude could have helped. In a roll-up of the "cons," by far the most frequently cited complaint was "little to no acknowledgment for a job well done."

Because this guy didn't realize, or give any weight to, the fact that his employees were desperate for some acknowledgment of their value, he missed a golden opportunity to better tap into their energy and talents.

One of the great ironies about this Time Myth is that leaders who believe it often have developed elaborate strategy documents, full of data analysis and projections about customer trends and market shifts, often bringing in outside consultants to fashion them—and paying dearly for that work. What they are overlooking are the insights that so many of their employees could bring. We have been privy to many such strategy plans, and we're usually asked to sign NDAs before looking at them. We respect the secrecy—we are outsiders after all—but what strikes us about this approach is that most often the strategy is kept confidential from anyone below the level of executive *inside* the company.

We point out that it's the employees who will be asked to do the work the strategy entails. Unfortunately, workers are so often treated as little more than afterthoughts in these documents beyond standard formulaic statements such as "Maintain an engaged workforce." Very little is included about how leadership actually intends to inspire their workers' hearts and minds to be engaged or execute on the strategy. Leadership teams are then surprised when they encounter employee resistance. Of course they do—they spend so little effort articulating this future vision to employees, and certainly very little getting employee feedback before committing to it. Clear strategy communication is essential to organizational alignment. If a plan doesn't get communicated to employees, how in the world will they understand their roles or how they can contribute to achieving them?

As Alan Mulally told us, "In most companies a few people

know the plan and leaders only share what they think others need to know. This is unheard of in business: But everyone needs to know the plan. And more importantly they need to know what the status is against the plan. You can't manage a secret."

Michael Mankins of Bain & Company, along with Richard Steele, wrote in the *Harvard Business Review* that companies on average deliver only 63 percent of the financial performance their strategies promise. They say this is often a result of overambition or changing markets, but too often it is from poor execution. Adds Balanced Scorecard expert and author Phil Jones, the main problem with execution is this: Typically only about 8 percent of an organization understands the strategy.

Gratitude Is a Two-Way Boulevard

What we are suggesting here is a mind shift. Instead of a productivity suck, gratitude must be seen as a multiplier. When it's done well, leaders become closer to their people and pay attention to what their employees are contributing, all of which opens the door for people to offer up concerns about problems they're seeing, ideas they've come up with, valuable information from customers and clients, and even mistakes they've made or problems they're running into with their work. All of this can be enormously useful for executing on the strategy and boosting performance.

We love the story former Netflix chief talent officer Patty

McCord tells about one hugely impactful question an employee asked that helped change the company's entire strategy. During an all-company meeting, Netflix's executive team was giving presentations about their parts of the business. After the chief content officer, Ted Sarandos, finished and opened the floor for questions, an engineer asked him why movies were released in so many steps—first to theaters, then to hotels, and then to cable services. Sarandos could very well have said, "That's the way it's always been done," but instead he considered the question. He realized the guy was smart and knew the formula, but the engineer was getting at something deeper. Sarandos answered honestly, "I don't know." He credits that question with prompting him to rethink the whole way content was released, which led to the Netflix system of putting up all episodes of a TV series at once. That, as we know, has led to the ginormous success of people bingeing Netflix shows. Just imagine the ROI on getting employees involved in that strategy discussion.

With the tools for expressing thanks we'll arm you with in Part II, managers can do a terrific job by devoting as little as one or two hours a week to the practice of gratitude.

Finding Time to Be Grateful

We don't suggest anyone has to add more hours into their days to fit in more thank-yous. What we do recommend to leaders is taking a hard look at all uses of time and doing a cost-benefit experiment. If you optimize efficiency across the board, how many minutes in your typical week might open up? An eye-opening study by professors Heike Bruch of the University of St. Gallen in Switzerland and Suman-tra Ghoshal of the London Business School suggests that for most leaders, there is plenty of slack to pick up. Over ten years of gathering data regarding time efficiency in nearly a dozen large companies, including Sony, LG Electronics, and Lufthansa, they found that only 10 percent of leaders were spending their time consistently in a committed, purposeful, and reflective manner.

Bruch and Ghoshal found that the most effective managers were more focused. They spent less time in reactive mode, not immediately responding to every issue that came up. They also found ways to cut down on distracting e-mails and meeting time. The researchers concluded that with this discipline, the most focused managers "can devote their full attention to the projects they believe in."

We appreciate what Gary Keller, author of *The ONE Thing*, has to say in this regard: "You need to be doing fewer things for more effect instead of doing more things with side effects."

Practicing gratitude offers the greatest effect for the time dedicated.

Chapter 5

Myth: I'm Not Wired to Feel It

With all we know about neuroscience and genetics, we have learned that some people are indeed naturally more inclined to be "warm and fuzzy" (though there are some important caveats we'll get to).

Research suggests there are very real differences in brain structure with people who tend to be more or less grateful. One such study found those naturally prone to feeling gratitude have more gray matter, or volume, in the part of the brain linked to interpreting others' intentions. Which means if we have a tendency to believe that the people we meet are helpful and kind, more out to help us than hurt us, then we will naturally be more thankful. Makes sense. Brains of more and less grateful people also show differences in *activity* levels. In a fascinating 2015 study, participants were asked to imagine they were Holocaust survivors who had received help from strangers. For example, they might be told, "A woman at the immigration agency stamps your passport so you can flee to England." The participants then rated how grateful they felt while researchers recorded what was going on in their noggins. People who reported feeling more gratitude showed amplified activity in two regions of the brain, both connected to emotional processing and interpersonal bonding; moral judgment; and the ability to understand the mental states of others. This suggests to us that those who innately feel more gratitude are also better able to connect with those around them, make ethical decisions, and be more sympathetic.

Our genes may well be involved in these neural differences, as our genetic makeup does lead to variations in people's general dispositions. One study compared the levels of gratitude commonly felt by identical twins (think the Property Brothers)—who essentially have the same DNA—versus fraternal twins (think Luke and Leia), who share only 50 percent of their DNA. Shouldn't be a shocker that the identical pairs felt much more similar levels of gratitude than did the fraternal. Other studies have suggested that specific genes underlie a naturally more or less grateful disposition. In one study, researchers asked each member of a married couple whether he/she, "thanked my partner for something that I appreciated" each night for a two-week period. Partners with one particular variant of a gene (CD38) thanked their partners more than 70 percent of the days, which, as you can imagine, is *waaaaay* more frequent than the population at large. Interestingly, that gene is involved in the secretion of oxytocin in the brain, one of the "happiness drugs."

Another suspect is a gene (COMT) that's involved in the circulation of dopamine in the brain, the so-called feel-good hormone associated with euphoria, bliss, motivation, and concentration. People with one variation of this gene reported feeling more grateful overall in life, while those with another variant felt less grateful. Researcher Dr. Jinping Liu suggests that people with the less grateful variant may be less sensitive to positive life events and more sensitive to the negative ones (what us non-scientists call "glass-half-empty people").

"These individuals may gradually form a habit of neglecting the positive aspects of life events and complaining about misfortunes—resulting in decreased positive personality traits such as gratitude and forgiveness," Liu writes—and we are all nodding because we know people like that. Adds executive coach Peter Bregman, author of *Leading with Emotional Courage*, "I think they don't feel gratitude for themselves, which makes it hard to feel gratitude for other people."

So, with all this research, why would we suggest "I'm not wired to feel grateful" is a myth? Because genetics and neuroscience have also shown that we are by no means slaves to our predispositions.

Genes Are Not Destiny

Our personalities and general temperaments are not set in stone. Once thought to be largely fixed after childhood, scientists now understand our brain structure has been shown to be pliable, or, as neuroscientists say, to have plasticity. That means it's no longer good enough to claim "I don't *do* gratitude." All of us can choose to practice behaviors that don't come naturally to us—like hugging in-laws—and by doing so, we can make them more natural.

David Gelles did groundbreaking work studying neuro-plasticity in London's taxi drivers. Required to memorize a complete map of the city's twisting, turning streets, not to mention learning shortcuts for when traffic became clogged, experienced London cabbies displayed substantially thicker gray matter of the hippocampus—an area associated with memory and spatial awareness—on scans than did the city's bus drivers, who follow the same route every day. A similar study of violinists, Gelles said, revealed that "parts of their brains associated with the motor mechanics of their left hands, used to hold the strings against the violin's neck, were far more developed than in non-violinists." Brains of people who speak a second language also feature more plasticity. Researchers conclude that becoming bilingual is possible because of functional changes in the brain even later in life. "The left inferior parietal cortex is larger in bilingual brains than in monolingual brains," writes Dr. Pascale Michelon of The Memory Practice.

We find that our brains adapt and even change according to our behavior throughout our lives. Scientists have a term they call "use-dependent cortical reorganization," which is a ten-dollar way of saying the neural pathways we use the most get stronger. As some neuroscientists say, "Neurons that fire together, wire together." (Not all of them say that, just the party-animal neuroscientists.)

So how can we start to rewire our brains toward gratitude? Says leadership expert and writer Vanessa Loder, "Imagine your brain has all these neural pathways connecting different responses." If an employee brings you a problem and you feel angry, that fires off a series of neurons. The same can occur with a tough situation with your kids or if you are stuck in rush hour congestion.

Adds Loder, "The first time you fire the sequence of 'Ugh, traffic, I'm angry,' it's as though you're walking through a jungle (in your brain), and you bushwhack a path and put a wooden plank across a stream. As you continue to have this same response, you strengthen the 'angry bridge.' The next thing you know, you've created a five-lane highway that makes it very easy to have an angry response. It's no longer a unique reaction to a unique stimulus, it is a habit."

She adds that if instead of feeling angry, a person were to turn their attention toward joy, compassion, and gratitude, they would start building a bridge that makes it easier to feel those feelings in the future. "The single wooden plank you lay down the first time you cultivate appreciation would become reinforced over time until you create a habitual response to feel compassion, gratitude, and appreciation without much conscious effort at all," she said.

Simply growing older can create positive personality changes like this, says Dr. Romeo Vitelli, a Canadian psychologist. As we mature, he argues, we usually become more agreeable and conscientious and develop greater emotional stability—as well as more gratitude for those around us.

Growing more comfortable with ourselves, our personalities can even change to match how we see ourselves.

If such changes can happen in the course of life without us doing diddly, just imagine how much we might be able to remold our personal dispositions by actually trying. Researchers conducted two studies, published in the *Journal of Personality and Social Psychology*, to see whether people could change measurable aspects of their personalities. In just sixteen weeks, people were able to significantly change their personalities, and this also corresponded to daily changes in their behavior.

Haven't we all had to stretch out of our comfort zones at work in one way or another? Maybe you had to become comfortable with giving public presentations or making small talk when networking—or being calm enough about those things to do a good job. When the two of us worked together in a large corporation years ago, Chester encouraged Adrian to get out of his comfort zone and have lunch with different groups of executives in the cafeteria a couple times a week. While Adrian would have naturally preferred to eat with his team—people he knew and liked—he ended up building important relationships by branching out.

In her marvelous book *Quiet*, Susan Cain writes about her struggle to combat a natural introversion when she was a lawyer. She found speaking up forcefully for her clients in meetings was difficult. She went on to give one of the most widely viewed TED Talks ever, making a case for giving the quiet and contemplative a voice in our organizations. She notes in her book that Rosa Parks, Eleanor Roosevelt, Al Gore, Warren Buffett, and even Mahatma Gandhi became major public figures despite being introverted (we would also add Piglet to the list).

The Power of (a Gratitude) Habit

In *The Power of Habit*, Charles Duhigg writes that habit is a coupling of a trigger that gets us to act followed by a routine that creates a reward. "For example, if we have a habit of eating an afternoon snack, the cue may be seeing a colleague head for the cafeteria, followed by the routine of joining him, which gives us the reward of a caffeine and sugar rush," says author Katherine Reynolds Lewis.

To change habits, we must replace undesired behaviors with more desirable ones. As such, we have seen many leaders coach themselves to make gratitude habitual. They tell themselves to watch for times when they can replace a behavior that's causing people to feel unappreciated with a gratitude-giving behavior. So, for example, when a salesperson e-mails asking for advice on a technical detail of a new contract, a manager might teach herself to take this as an opportunity to also express gratitude to the person for winning this tough deal in the first place and paying such close attention to the particulars.

In short, if you're disposed to think you're just not cut out for expressing gratitude—that it doesn't come naturally, at least not at work—then give yourself some credit. You absolutely can get the hang of it. It might feel a little strange at first, and perhaps forced. "Who wants to receive my rote praise?" leaders may complain. But once they start putting a little effort into the practice, they see that even if they're a tad awkward, people still respond quite well.

Even leaders who aren't especially comfortable with this practice can pick it up fairly quickly, says David Ulrich, University of Michigan professor and cofounder of The RBL Group. He explained to us that gratitude and other softer skills such as empathy, listening, and creating meaning often do not match leaders' unconscious models of effective leadership—where "to lead" means being in front and in charge. Ulrich says, "We must get a mind-set that leaders empower others to lead. This happens when we get inside others' heads; when we observe, listen, ask, encourage, and communicate sincere appreciation for what they have done."

We love the story *Inc.* magazine president and CEO Eric Schurenberg told us about how he learned the value of gratitude when working as a young reporter at *Time.* "I had a stereotypical curmudgeon editor as a boss, and when I transferred out of his group into a better job, I took the time to express gratitude to him. To me it was an observation of a truth: I would never have had this other opportunity if I had not worked for him. But he was so moved. This flinty, grumpy guy just melted, and I realized this gratitude thing is really powerful!"

Gratitude is a mighty force, and no matter how we are wired, we can make it part of who we are.

Chapter 6

Myth: I Save My Praise
for Those Who Deserve It

When we suggested to one manager that he express gratitude to a lower-level employee who we could see felt unappreciated, the leader quipped back: "Why? A monkey could do his job." That's an extreme case of cluelessness, but the guy *was* memorable!

Managers who believe the "I save my praise" myth withhold their gratitude because they harbor a fundamental disrespect for some types of work and some workers. To these folks, everyone is just a number.

As the television show *Undercover Boss* showcased, the value being added by many people on a manager's own team and in support functions around the company is often overlooked or discounted. We've found that whole departments are commonly left out when it comes to who gets credit for success. In a sales-driven company, for example, we typically see little appreciation for the people in, say, billing, even though without them sales are not fully made. It's likewise uncommon in an operations-focused organization, such as a construction company, to see people in marketing rewarded, for example, even though they do a lot to burnish the brand and help land the big deal everyone is working on.

As for the so-called basic support jobs, what we especially like about *Undercover Boss* is that it shows how freakin' hard such work can be, not to mention how important the jobs are to actual customers. As that realization dawns on the executives—who are struggling to make a pizza to specifications in just minutes or sorting recycling for an eight-hour shift all while wearing a fake beard and Mr. Magoo's spectacles—they are not only humbled but filled with gratitude for the talent and fortitude so many unsung heroes bring to their jobs day-in and day-out.

Here is one example that might help turn this kind of thinking around. It's from the research team of University of Michigan professors Amy Wrzesniewski and Jane Dutton, who led a study of custodians in a hospital in the Midwest. You'd probably agree that janitors are out of the sight line of most executives. In their study, the researchers found a staff member, Candice Philipps, who was seen as particularly kind by patients and families and made a big difference in their stays at the hospital. The researchers interviewed Philipps, whose job it was to clean up vomit and excrement in the oncology ward as patients came in for chemotherapy. At the lowest point they can imagine, when they are physically ill, emotionally embarrassed, and afraid, this custodian showed up with a mop, a bucket, and a kindly smile and put them at ease.

She said of her work, "At their lowest and most vulnerable point, I help them maintain their dignity. I make it okay to feel awful, to lose control. My role is crucial in the healing process."

Holy smokes. Is it ever—as anyone who has been in that unfortunate situation or has had a loved one go through it can attest. Can you imagine a worker like Philipps in your organization? One gets the feeling that no matter where she worked, she would find meaning and wow her clients. Is there any doubt that she deserves gratitude?

We all understand the damage that can occur when various "simple" jobs are done poorly. Who hasn't had a miserable customer service rep answer the phone, or a hard-nosed banker deny our request, or a fast-food worker who mumbles dutifully "Have a nice day" without a trace of conviction?

You also never know which employee might make a vital observation that stops a problem before it develops or go that extra step to please a client, keeping that customer instead of losing them to a competitor. Managers can't monitor all of the many daily moments at work. Doesn't it, then, behoove leaders to take advantage of gratitude as a positive way to boost motivation and encourage people to do the best they can with every task?

Debunking the Pareto Principle

A worry some leaders have within this myth is the idea of favoritism. They are concerned that they are going to naturally praise certain people on the team more than others—since those workers are high achievers—and the others will be jealous. "He's just the teacher's pet," employees will grumble. It's true that many workers might not have access to the full skinny on each team member's performance, so they might see disproportionate praise as biased. A few thoughts on this. First, some people are going to be recognized more than others. That's just a fact. It's a manager's job to ensure that gratitude is specific and public, so everyone understands why it's happening. Second, it's also a manager's job to ensure everyone on the team gets a chance to receive gratitude at some point. It might not be completely equal, but everyone should get a chance to be in the spotlight now and then. This is best achieved when managers take the time to find out what everyone is working on—i.e., is an employee covering for another, is someone mentoring a new person, and so on.

Named after Italian economist Vilfredo Pareto, the Pareto Principle suggests that 80 percent of "effects" typically come from 20 percent of "causes." In business, it's been interpreted to suggest that 20 percent of our tasks account for 80 percent of our results, so we should pare out as much of the other 80 percent as we can. It's also been used to argue that 20 percent of team members generally contribute about 80 percent of overall team performance.

While many leaders buy into the Pareto Principle when assessing talent—and argue that star performers can account for a disproportionate amount of earnings, productivity, and innovative ideas—they often miss the fact that they have a large number of people whose performance is comparatively average (or lackluster). Isn't it a given, then, that by inspiring this bigger group to improve their performance, the team could see a substantial overall increase? There's a fundamental logical flaw in the notion that a leader's gratitude should only be offered to those who are in important positions doing exceptional work.

So what about those who are underperforming? Our argument: Gratitude for things they do well, on time, and to expectations can have a catalytic effect on their morale and motivation, and therefore their overall results. A few managers have argued back with us that employees who do average work are probably not going to step up their games—it's in their natures to do what's acceptable and nothing more. In most of those cases, we think, the spark of their natural inner drives has been muted from years of invisibility. The effects of offering thanks for their contributions can be extraordinary.

Don't take our word for it. Consider this story that Schon Beechler, now a revered professor at INSEAD (the number-three-ranked business school in the world), tells about appreciation she received for a basic contribution in a low-level job at the beginning of her working life. Her first job was at a plastics factory in New York, where she started on the simplest machine and moved her way up to working a complicated injection mold. Each machine was operated by one person, so there was no one to talk with, and after a few weeks the foreman realized this sharp new employee was becoming bored and disengaged.

"One afternoon he assigned me to a machine at the back of the factory that made the plastic red lenses that are inserted in stoplights," Beechler recalls. "He said in a quiet voice, 'You know, this job is really important. When you do a good job, the plastic in this lens reflects the light behind it just right so that drivers can see the red signal when they pull up to the stoplight. Doing the best-quality job on this machine will help to save many people's lives. I think you have had enough experience on the other machines that I can trust you.'" Genius.

All these years later, Beechler describes this moment as though it just happened. Her supervisor's trust meant the world to her, and she promised she would do her best. This manager made her feel important, and she was determined to live up to his praise. His gratitude for her fundamental contribution and his expression of belief in the skill it entailed helped transform a dull job into one of meaning, "giving me energy, focus, and commitment to my job that was completely lacking when all I could see was another monotonous task," she said.

What's more, that lift of motivation required nothing but a little generosity of spirit on the part of the leader. A simple yet sincere approach anyone can master.

A point: You never know who's going to be your next superstar. As he was working his way up, retired American Express chairman Ken Chenault told us, "The best recognition I received was when someone said to me, 'I trust your judgment, and you can make that decision.' Another type of recognition I really valued is when someone said, 'Here's how an act of yours made an impact on me.'"

As we find, gratitude is not a zero-sum game—there is plenty to go around. The admiration we have for high-performing people and important roles doesn't have to come at the expense of others on the team. One of the things that's most remarkable about gratitude is that even when it's expressed about the simplest tasks, it has outsize impact.

Chapter 7

Myth: It's All about the Benjamins

We hear from many bosses who believe the only truly meaningful expression of gratitude they could offer is padding employees' wallets with raises and bonuses. This is a tricky issue, because money absolutely matters—it's what separates us from the animals . . . that and hats. So it's vital to pay people appropriately. In struggling cultures, we often find employees doing work of a higher pay grade than they're rewarded for, or that bonuses are so complicated that a gaggle of astrophysicists couldn't explain the formulas. Ofttimes employees can't benefit from financial rewards, due not to their own performance but to business challenges well beyond their control—competitive pressures, regulatory issues, or product failures that torpedo the year. "You crushed it this year, Val. Really amazing work. But our factory in Nepal missed its quota, so no bonus."

Of course, financial results have to tie to overall organizational performance—we are all part of a bigger team, but, say Bill Fotsch and John Case writing in *Forbes*, the "trouble is, at most companies, employees have no idea how the business is doing or whether they're likely to get a bonus. If it comes, it's like manna from heaven. If it doesn't, people feel cheated."

These authors point to a bonus structure that they found highly effective at a fast-growing Los Angeles company called One Week Bath. Every week the entire workforce sees a spreadsheet showing year-to-date net profit (which earns them their bonus) and exactly how much they have made to date. They also get a chance to see the forecast profit and bonus for the rest of the year. Results are shared—good or bad—every Wednesday in a thirty-minute meeting.

Say Fotsch and Case, "What distinguishes this bonus? It's objective, it doesn't depend on some executive's assessment of performance. It's wholly transparent. It's generous (it would equal six weeks of wages the year they studied the company). It's self-funding—the increase in profits is substantially more than the cost of the bonus."

In our experience, the best bonus structures use these kinds of elements and are based on a combination of organizational, unit, and individual performance. They are intended to help people understand the connection between their work and financial rewards.

With pay levels so transparent these days (thanks to the miracle of the Internet and the refreshing demand for transparency from millennials), it's important to rectify imbalances and respond to employee requests for compensation conversations in a respectful, forthright way. A young friend of ours is currently looking for a new job, despite being promoted three times in two years at a booming tech startup. When she's asked for raises to go along with her added responsibilities, the response from her manager has been, in her words, "blumbering" (which is millennial for "mumbling BS").

Pay inequities can dissatisfy. No way around that.

That being said, there is usually only so much money to go around. While gratitude is not a zero-sum game, by contrast, compensation almost always is. If someone gets a big raise, then others on the team usually are balanced out with less. And we know those decisions can be extremely hard for a leader. That's especially true when you know your people are just about killing themselves to hit their goals—sometimes unrealistic ones that were dictated from above. All this makes gratitude all the more meaningful.

We want to be 100 percent clear that we are not suggesting that gratitude can substitute for appropriate compensation. A thoughtful and timely thank-you card won't cover anyone's monthly payment on their Kia. What we do want to emphasize is that using monetary rewards alone does not motivate people—at least not for long—and it can even backfire. As we found at one large company we visited, employees and managers complained about the elaborate bonus structure that promised riches. Workers, however, felt the company did not provide the support necessary to hit their numbers—so everyone ended up hating the system and no one knew of any employee who had hit the jackpot.

Why Cash Doesn't Pack a Punch

Focus on monetary rewards alone can create a mercenary environment in which people will leave for a little more at the drop of a hat. Some of the highest-paying companies we've studied have insane turnover rates. The highest turnover industry today is technology—with attrition rates exceeding that of retail. And the number one reason these valuable programmers and network administrators are jumping ship? Compensation. When you create a culture in which comp is king, it will be.

In our consulting work, we've found another reason monetary rewards usually don't pack a punch of deeply felt gratitude: The rewards are few and far between and often come during annual reviews, so they are seen as a matter of management process rather than an expression of sincere gratitude for valued work. Research on cash and cash-equivalent bonuses will surprise bosses who consider these bonuses powerful motivators. When we've asked employees how they spent their last windfall from work, their number one response is "paid bills," and number two is "I don't remember."

We believe targeted and meaningful awards can be extremely powerful. While working as a manager in the corporate world, one of us wished to reward a fantastic employee after a project launch. He asked the CEO for permission. The employee and her husband were building a new home, which gave him an idea of rewarding her with much-needed power tools to provide sweat equity. He knew she'd love the gift. The CEO said an expenditure on a reward of that type would not be permitted, but he did say he'd approve a raise at the end of the year—five months away. So what could have been a touching, memorable way to show gratitude for remarkable work turned into just another performance review ritual.

Research shows that monetary rewards alone have a limited effect on motivation and, by extension, performance—especially once an employee has reached a comfortable level of income. Our Motivators Assessment data of seventy-five thousand people shows "money" comes in dead last in a ranking of the twenty-three most common motivators, and that's for people in their sixties down to those in their twenties. Only 10 percent of people overall have money in their top seven of the twenty-three motivators. Compensation for most people is what we call a threshold issue. In other words, once an employee crosses the threshold and earns a level of compensation that enables her to pay the bills, then factors other than how much she makes become more motivating.

A separate 2012 study by German and Swiss researchers found tangible items, like the above-mentioned rejected power tools reward, were far more motivating to employees than cash bonuses. What was most motivating was knowing that their bosses appreciated their efforts. That had the most lasting effect on motivation.

Another trouble with monetary rewards as gratitude is that some goals can't be tied to a number. In some cases, assigning a metric might be crude and actually devalue the effort and the meaning of the work. Putting a dollar figure to the completion of a stretch project, for instance, can confuse an employee or even demotivate her if she's put a lot of time and effort into the assignment or believes it has more significant implications for the company's success than the few hundred dollars that come in her next check. In addition, some work just doesn't lend itself to the kinds of measurement that so many compensation and bonus plans use. Even in sales, a number of units sold might not reflect how tough a job a salesperson has been assigned. One sales team was giving new reps nightmare patchwork territories to sell in to—with all the best client companies given to veteran salespeople in other areas. With quarterly rankings available for all to see in the dashboard, new salespeople were losing their minds trying to keep up. Most quit after just a few quarters.

One more challenge with cash bonuses is that some employees tend to game the program when money is involved, finding ways around the rules and trying to fix the odds in their favor. We were once asked to speak to the sales group of a large technology company. While chatting with one of the top performers in a meet-and-greet, he told us he'd made his bonus only the week before by selling a new solution to a client. "That's good news," we said. "What's the client using the product for?"

His reply, "Don't know, don't care."

When cash rules, people too often focus on the prize instead of doing what's best for their customers.

In recent history, few instances illustrate this better than when Wells Fargo CEO Tim Sloan credited a bonus structure with leading thousands of employees to secretly create unauthorized banking and credit card accounts without their customers' knowledge. "We had an incentive plan in our retail banking group that drove inappropriate behavior," he said candidly. The bogus accounts allowed employees to boost their sales figures and make more money.

Of course we are not suggesting that compensation and bonuses shouldn't be tied to performance. Such programs that are well crafted can have a satisfying effect on the entire workforce. But when all rewards are focused on numbers, and when all rewards are in cash, then a company and its people can lose their way.

Thoughtful organizations complement important discussions about compensation by also considering the more qualitative contributions of employees and balancing criticism with heartfelt appreciation.

Chapter 8

Myth: They'll Think I'm Bogus

*H*ow can I just come in one day and be this new person—*handing out gratitude right and left?* We've heard variations on this question, and we get where the concern is coming from. If a boss has been so busy that he's been heads-down, holed up in his office all the time or constantly away in meetings and then all of a sudden shows up by their desks patting their backs and giving out thanks like cigars from a new father, who wouldn't wonder what's going on? We also hear concerns that, as one manager told us, "I'd look like I'm trying to manipulate them." That could be true if your gratitude isn't genuine (more on that in a bit).

About the first point—the transforming boss—we can say that unless there is a complete lack of trust in a team (which is rare, and if you were that kind of leader, you wouldn't have made it this far into this book), managers can be confident that employees will appreciate a change of this kind, no matter how neglectful or hard-nosed they've acted in the past. Humans are generally supportive of other people's efforts to make positive changes in behavior, especially if it benefits them.

Frankly, it's part of human makeup to root for people who want to grow and change, even, and perhaps especially, our bosses. We love to watch transformations. Gordon Ramsay has built an empire on the premise, and HGTV has an entire network dedicated to it. Just about every popular movie features someone who transforms—from Katniss Everdeen to *Shrek's* Fiona. Just think about Marty McFly changing from a high school goof-off to a time-traveling hero pretty much overnight in *Back to the Future*. "I guess these kinds of things happen when parents let their kids hang out with a weird old man in his garage. Time travel is actually the best possible outcome for that scenario, when you think about it," quipped actor David Christopher Bell.

As human beings we are designed to give people who are trying to make positive life changes the benefit of the doubt. An important point here for leaders is to be up-front with their teams about how they've realized a change is due. Showing more gratitude is a form of respect, and any time a leader conveys that they want to be sure they're showing due respect to the team it is going to be well received. Openly acknowledging past negligence or harshness, or sharing that they've been so focused on trying to keep up with a punishing schedule that they may have been taking out their stress on the team, is part of the process. True, it might not be easy to say, but the honesty will be prized by those in their care.

As our friend Marshall Goldsmith says, a change like this

will take courage, humility, and discipline. Courage, he says, is all about looking in the mirror, getting out of your comfort zone, and being vulnerable as you try new things. He puts it beautifully when he says, "There is no comfort in the change zone and no change in the comfort zone." As to humility, he emphasizes that it's a hallmark of the best managers. Jim Collins famously found that the strongest managers he studied for his classic *Good to Great*—whom he called Level 5 Leaders—displayed a powerful mixture of personal humility and indomitable will. While incredibly ambitious, their ambition was first and foremost for the cause, the organization, and its purpose—not themselves.

Hubert Joly, retired CEO of Best Buy, made a fascinating connection between making changes to his leadership style and adopting a new orientation toward graciousness and approachability. He told us, "What really helped me change as a leader, and learn the importance of gratitude, was to start seeing everyone as my customer—our team is my customer, my board is my customer . . . my waiter is my customer. Our natural tendency is to treat a customer well."

The Authenticity Challenge

Worrying about how we'll be perceived as we go through a transformation like this is part of the human condition; it's woven into the fabric of our being. But the irony is that when we're trying to control how others see us, *that's* when we usually come across as inauthentic. We also cut ourselves off

from important insights into how we're actually being perceived. If leaders could see themselves on film, tracking the
way their teams see them, many of them would be stunned.
It would not be a leap to realize that, clearly, their team members would be receptive to a change, even if it doesn't at first
seem the most natural thing in the world.

In short, it's actually preferred for a manager to explain to
their direct reports that they want to make sure they're doing
a better job of showing their gratitude. The key is whether or
not the intent is genuine, and whether or not they stick with
it. In emphasizing that discipline is a necessity for making
authentic change, Goldsmith says that means sticking with
the new course taken as you inevitably encounter difficulties.

Think about it: How many conversations have you had
with friends and loved ones about a boss they wish would
change? Imagine one day they say, "He *finally* told me I do
a good job with my presentations. It's about time!" Will it
take some convincing that the manager is being genuine and
really making a change? Almost surely. But pretty soon their
shock will fade once showing gratitude becomes a regular
occurrence. We've seen that people can be incredibly generous with their appreciation of being appreciated. The whole
tenor and energy level of a team can be transformed remarkably quickly.

We met with one leader who told us he'd made a dramatic
turnaround about the value of expressing gratitude. Founder
and chairman of one of the most successful content marketing firms in the country, Likeable Media, Dave Kerpen told

us he started out as a gratitude cynic early in his career. "Anything that sounds too good to be true I'm going to be skeptical of," he told us. "How in the world would a feeling like gratitude impact my business or make me more money? It doesn't make sense. But I kept hearing about gratitude three, four, or five times from people I knew were successful and I respected. I thought I at least needed to give it a shot."

In conducting research for his book *Likeable Business*, Kerpen talked to more than two hundred CEOs. "I was amazed," he said. "The most common theme I heard was the practice of gratitude. The founder of Restaurant.com said he starts his day by making a list of the things and people he's grateful for. Sheldon Yellen, CEO of BELFOR, writes gratitude notes to his employees every year on their birthday, which is amazing since he has more than fifty thousand employees. He's writing a couple dozen handwritten notes every single day. It was practices like those that got me thinking there's got to be something here. And it's what helped me start focusing on gratitude in my own life."

It's a practice that has paid off. Not only is Likeable Media one of the city's fastest-growing marketing firms, but it has been named a Best Place to Work in New York four years in a row.

No Strings Attached

Regarding the worry that people will think you're trying to manipulate them, there's a simple rule: Don't attach strings.

Some leaders we've worked with have said they think people will see it as a kind of verbal bribery to serve the interests of the person offering it. We've probably all experienced a boss thanking us in that spirit. "Terrific work on the Rimsky account, Sue, now I'd like you to take on a couple of even bigger deals!" That tactic can even work—for a while. Employees who feel flattered do sometimes fall into the trap of being happily overloaded. But that is horrible management. Not only will those people eventually be ground down into pulp, but they will realize they've been taken advantage of. And the news of the leaders' tactics will spread as fast as a wildfire, or today, a retweet of an Instagram video of a wildfire. Soon colleagues will be well aware of that person's leadership style.

Expressing authentic gratitude is about much more than *what* a leader says, or even *how* she says it—it's about *why* she says it. Most people are quite sensitive to that. So, on the positive side of this coin, if you're being genuine—even if it's unexpected and your delivery style seems a little stilted at first—people are going to pick up on your sincerity. After all, you will be recognizing behaviors that you value, and that is the first step in ensuring sincerity.

One more issue regarding authenticity that should be addressed. Some managers have told us that they've had people on their team whom they frankly just don't like. They find giving them praise uncomfortable. They also expect that if they did, except in the most obvious cases of their having done a really special job, that person would be incredulous. Well, not to be too technical here, but tough noogies. When a leader doesn't like an employee, that employee is usually fairly well aware of it. We understand the concern. All managers will face this problem at some point in their careers. The thing to keep in mind here is that showing gratitude at work isn't about developing a friendship. It's about you developing professional leadership skills. You've got to get over your bad self and learn to reward people for every step they take forward, and not their personalities. With the advice we give in the second part of the book, even in the trickiest of cases, managers will know how to express gratitude that is sincere and appreciated with all of their people.

That's where we go next.

Part II

The Eight Most Powerful
Gratitude Practices

It's time to get to work.

In this part of the book we identify the eight most effective approaches we've found for showing gratitude in our work with leaders around the world. We've seen that as managers adopt these
behaviors, their people find them authentic and motivating—and
there's usually a corresponding uptick in morale and engagement.

We group these concepts into two categories: seeing and
expressing.

Seeing involves ways leaders can ensure they'll spot great work
being done, and expressing covers the best ways we've seen
managers voice and show their thanks.

We hope you'll want to adopt some of these practices right
away, so feel free to pick and choose those that are most appeal-
ing to you. There's no need to try to tackle everything at once,
and the specific recipe of ideas that will work best is going to be

different for each individual. Figuring it out is part of the fun. Find a few ways that are most natural to you, and perhaps one or two that require you to stretch.

As you'll see, the leaders we introduce you to in these chapters have been remarkably innovative in their approaches. They've told us they love finding little things they can do that are simple but mean so much to their people.

These managers derive a great sense of joy from their gratitude practices, and we know you will too.

Seeing

Chapter 9

Solicit and Act on Input

Henry David Thoreau may have been speaking up for employees when he wrote, "The greatest compliment anyone gave me was when they asked me for my opinion and then attended to my answer."

Shortly after we'd started working with the leader of one manufacturing firm, we were fortunate to be on site as he brought his two thousand employees together one day to explain the hard reality of the company's situation: Sales were down, expenses were up, and competitors were disrupting with innovative solutions and faster delivery. In an exceptional display of humility, he admitted he needed their help. "I will tell you how we're going to save this company," he said. "I don't know. But if human ingenuity can bring about a miracle, then we're going to do it. And I will do everything in my power to accomplish it. But my power doesn't include all the ideas or all the ingenuity or all the working together that we need. My brain doesn't contain all the answers, but

I'll know a good one when I hear it. And I'll be grateful to that person.

"Our future is in your heads collectively. Together, we can be Albert Einstein; we can be geniuses. What do you say, can we do it?"

The employees cheered, and everyone started milling back to their workstations. Unfortunately, that's too often where such good intentions end, but this leader immediately began showing that he was serious. He spent hours every day walking through the office cubicle maze and throughout the cells of the factory floor. He asked smart questions. He listened. His office door was never closed, not once.

And ideas started coming in, albeit tentatively at first. He called us after a couple of burly guys in overalls came into his office rather sheepishly and asked if they could pitch a concept that might cut production through-time in their manufacturing cell. The CEO was thrilled, began publicizing efforts like that one, recognized the idea generators in public celebrations, and soon ideas started pouring in. The result? In the three years after that speech, his seventy-five-year-old company cut product manufacturing time from two weeks to six hours, and they grew sales by more than 20 percent while actually reducing costs and headcount through attrition.

Of course, the advice to actively solicit input from employees is not new, but in our work we have rarely seen managers doing it. Even more rare is to see them follow through on suggestions. Let's face it, many ideas won't be viable, and yes, some people might get upset if their contributions aren't acted upon if you don't explain why. But openly discussing with them the reasons their ideas are not feasible and conveying authentic appreciation for the input assures them you've given thoughtful consideration.

When we discuss this idea with managers, we've found that many are leery. Some tell us, "Oh, employees always think they know how to fix the business, but they don't really understand the issues." Well, consider this a great opportunity to actually communicate with employees to fill them in about aspects of the organization, the marketplace and industry, and constraints they may not be aware of.

For instance, a factory manager we were speaking with told us how an employee of his in the accounting department had suggested their business should be opened for school groups to visit as a way to build interest with potential future workers. The manager had assumed that every one of his people would know why that was a terrible idea: The company used toxic chemicals (including cyanide for electroplating), and the risk in bringing children into the building was too great. He explained this at his next all-hands meetings, and was surprised to find that not only his bookkeepers but many others hadn't understood the issue. One employee said, "We thought you were worried about people stealing stuff."

As an endnote, this manager told us he continued to mull this discussion over, and finally, with help from a cross-functional team of employees, he was able to open the factory to the public a couple of Saturdays a year with carefully orchestrated tours led by employee volunteers. On the day of the first tour, the line stretched around the block. No one got hurt, nothing got stolen, and the community got a chance to see the innovative things his team was building.

Another common objection to soliciting ideas is "I don't want my people preoccupied with what's wrong. They're already too negative. They need to stop kvetching and get their jobs done!" Sure, we can't deny that's a valid concern, but it is also a manager's responsibility to ensure employees focus their ideas on specific *positive* solutions that the team can actually implement.

Line Dancing and a Better Mac and Cheese

A leader we have long admired for his ability to cull positive ideas from employees is Kent Taylor, founder, CEO, and chairman of Texas Roadhouse. The company has almost six hundred restaurants and is one of the casual dining industry's most profitable concepts. And Texas Roadhouse doesn't spend a dime on major media advertising. It doesn't need to.

Their secret to success? "As a leader, you get your ass out of the office and go visit the people in the stores, or wherever you have your business," Taylor told us. "And when you see a great idea, you write that person a note and thank them. I must have sent thirty notes already this month."

Taylor is quick to credit the company's growth to his team of nearly sixty thousand strong. He listens to these folks, he says, because no one gave him the time of day when he was working his way up. At a fried chicken chain Taylor worked at early in his career, "I got in trouble for trying to show them what the future looked like with chicken sandwiches, chicken fingers, stuff like that we didn't have at the time. They said, basically, 'We're good.'"

But Texas Roadhouse has benefited from voices everywhere. One thing the chain is known for is line dancing, where servers and hosts perform impromptu boot-scootin' routines to country music that blasts out now and then throughout the night. That idea came from one rogue store manager. Said Taylor, "When I had about twenty stores, my head of operations says, 'Hey, there's an operator in Kentucky who's breaking the rules. He's got line dancing going on.' I went and checked it out, and it was cool. So I spread that idea to everybody else at the company."

Every one of the store operators has Taylor's cell number, and they aren't afraid to use it. "I got a call recently from one of our area managers," Taylor told us. "We serve mac and cheese on our kids' menu, and his daughter had created this little book about why she thought our mac and cheese sucks. We are now having the restaurants in his market test a new made-from-scratch mac and cheese. I thought it was cool that he felt safe enough to send me that."

Taylor also actively seeks feedback, especially from those working directly with customers. On many Sunday nights (after the weekend rush) he'll call stores at random and ask to talk to half a dozen servers and ask if guests like or dislike new menu items. When he visits a restaurant, his first stop is with the servers, then he makes his way to the meat room, then the kitchen line, and finally to the store manager. "I know if the manager is full of s*** or not by then because I've already talked to the other people," he said.

Texas Roadhouse is thriving, its people are engaged, and customers are happy. Taylor says, "It's not rocket science: We put our people number one, the guest is number two; how we treat our employees reflects on how our employees treat our guests." Yee-haw!

Avoiding Over-asks

We're not saying there aren't potential downsides in soliciting ideas. A few of them are the leader's own dang fault, such as the manager we met who tried to get down in the trenches with his people, but instead of finding ideas to act upon, he ended up criticizing more. Behind his back, his people began calling him the Seagull for his tendency to drop in just long enough to dump on everyone and then leave.

As we coach leaders, we try to provide guidelines for getting this right. One of the first suggestions is to avoid the "over-ask"—expecting too much from employees with questions out of their purview (e.g., "How can we solve our pricing problems?") Only a few people in your entire organization would have ideas about solving something so complex, and that kind of ask might make people feel diminished. Another problem with the over-ask, says innovation writer Hutch Carpenter, is asking too many questions at once. For example, he once heard a leader ask this question: "How might we become more competitive? Think in terms of new revenue sources, increased efficiencies, non-value-added work, margin enhancements, etc." Carpenter's critique: "Revenue. Operational efficiency. Bureaucracy. Margins. All in one question. It even includes 'etc.,' which is essentially asking for everything but the kitchen sink."

Another guideline: Make sure the "specificity fits," so that you ask the right question to the right people in the right way. For instance, "How can we reduce fuel consumption while we are making deliveries?" is a question focused to solicit ideas to cut gasoline costs from anyone even remotely involved in the process of sending your goods out the door. However, asking: "How can we improve the way we deliver our products to customers?" may be more apt if you are hoping for more out-there, blue-sky solutions to improving your transportation service. Both can be effective ways of soliciting ideas, but one or the other will work better depending on whether your needs and expectations are specific (cutting fuel costs) or more general (how we can "wow" when making deliveries). And we've found if there's a free pizza lunch associated with asking these or any questions, response rates will rise miraculously.

Getting Good Ideas

We've witnessed leaders achieve resounding successes when they solicit and act on advice, but this doesn't have to be a formal process or add time to already busy days. One case we found was that of Quint Studer, who gained a reputation as a turnaround artist when he was administrator of the 492-bed Baptist Hospital in Pensacola, Florida.

When he started in that role, rather than parking next to the front door in the administrator's reserved spot, Studer decided to always park in the farthest lot. That way he would have the opportunity to talk to an employee or two every morning on the long walk to the building. He also made daily rounds of the facility, introducing himself: "Hi, my name is Quint. I'm the new administrator here. I work for you. What should I do today?" He told us that from the way people looked at him, he suspected many were going to suggest "Take a urine screen."

One day a nurse opened up and said, "Tonight, when I leave, it's going to be dark. We work in a pretty tough neighborhood. I park out by the bushes, and they haven't been trimmed in months. I worry that when I go out to my car someone could be hiding there. Could you get those bushes trimmed?" During the next twelve hours, while she was working her shift, Studer had the bushes clipped and was even able to have maintenance put up a small fence. The nurse was not only impressed but deeply gratified, and she shared those feelings with her colleagues.

Her story and others spread around the company, and people came to understand that Studer was going to respect their input and act on it if he could. Suggestions began rushing in, and remarkable things happened. Employees began to up their games. Patient satisfaction—which previously had ranged between the 9th and 40th percentiles—soared to the 99th percentile of hospitals nationally. Turnover dropped by 18 percent, and the organization's financials became rock solid. Moody's upgraded the bond rating of the hospital, and Baptist was ranked in the hundred best places to work in the country by *Fortune* magazine.

Thankfully the experience at Baptist Hospital is not an anomaly in the organizations we study. Every day workers will face challenges in their work, and each of those problems can spark ideas for improvements. The best leaders harvest those ideas to enhance performance. At Amazon, for instance, the company's intranet features an online suggestion box for employees to propose anything they think will make the company better, which is how free shipping was first suggested by software engineer Charlie Ward. That idea emerged in the insanely popular Prime program. British Airways launched a virtual idea box of its own, asking for employee help to reduce emissions and cut fuel bills. One "out-there" idea was to reduce the weight of their planes by descaling toilet pipes (don't ask—you don't want to know), an idea that has cut fuel bills by almost one million dollars each year.

A Virtuous Circle

Soliciting ideas and considering them thoughtfully is not only a great way to find improvements, it also can raise morale. Why? The right approach to idea generation creates a virtuous circle, say Alan Robinson and Dean Schroeder, professors at the University of Massachusetts Amherst and Valparaiso University. Their research has found workers become more engaged when they see ideas from employees being used. And managers, seeing the impact of their workers' ideas, tend to give their people more authority—which leads to more and better ideas.

They point to Japanese petroleum company Idemitsu, which gets, on average, more than a hundred ideas per employee each year without offering any bonuses for the ideas. After all, monetary-based reward plans for innovation, such as offering a percentage of the savings or profits from each idea, can turn out to be counterproductive, creating an enormous amount of non-value-added work and also undermining teamwork and trust. Success also can be stalled when idea programs require multiple levels of approval or when simple tools for submitting ideas aren't provided to employees.

Idemitsu and other innovative organizations have found that most employees have lots of ideas and take pride in contributing to the organization's success. You could say they have a yen to contribute. The most effective form of recognition for such ideas is when their leaders are able to implement them quickly and give credit, not cash, to the employees involved.

Solicit and Act on Input

+ Actively soliciting input from employees is not a new concept, but few managers do it well.

+ While some ideas won't be viable, and a few employees might get upset if their contributions aren't used, openly discussing the reasons their ideas are not feasible and conveying authentic appreciation for input assures workers a leader has given thoughtful consideration.

+ Avoid the over-ask—expecting too much from employees by asking for ideas that are out of their purview or asking too many questions at once.

+ Ensure specificity fits—so the right question is asked of the right people in the right way. General questions (e.g., How can we better "wow" when making deliveries?) allow for open-ended suggestions and blue-sky brainstorming, while more specific inquiries (e.g., How can we cut our fuel costs?) work better if a leader is seeking answers to a more precise need.

+ Soliciting and acting upon ideas can raise morale. Research has found workers become more engaged when they see employee ideas being used, and managers, seeing the impact, tend to give their people more authority.

+ Monetary-based reward plans for ideas can turn out to be counterproductive. Innovation can also be stalled when idea programs require multiple levels of approval or when simple tools for submitting ideas are not provided.

Chapter 10

Assume Positive Intent

We wish we had a dime for every time a leader said to us something to the effect of "Some days it seems like I'm the only one around here who can do anything right!" They then regale us with examples of mistakes their people make. Some indeed are head-scratchers, like workers driving the company truck who flip off other drivers on the freeway, or waiters who can't seem to go a single day without breaking something, or office workers who are compelled to hit reply all to every friggin' e-mail that comes their way—most often just to say thanks or send a smiley face emoji.

Let's accept that all of us can do some pretty boneheaded things now and then.

But quite often there are innocent enough reasons things have gone wrong that leaders aren't aware of or haven't paid attention to. They jump to the assumption that employees are being careless, aren't applying themselves, or are as bright as brine shrimp. Some leaders even assume there's malevolent intent afoot with each mistake, as if their employees are trying to undermine them.

Our work interviewing employees over decades has helped us understand that the vast majority of people do care about their work and are trying to do a good job. Almost no one clocks in wanting to fail. All too frequently employee performance is hampered by a key set of factors largely out of their control, such as the lack of proper tools, thorough training, and clear direction, which might be due to changing priorities or confusing explanations on the part of the leader.

We admire what Indra Nooyi, retired chairman and CEO of PepsiCo, said when asked for the most important leadership advice she had been given: "Whatever anybody says or does, assume positive intent. When you follow this advice, your whole approach to a person or problem becomes very different."

When leaders conversely assume negative intent, they can quickly become angry or annoyed by those who bring them problems. "If you let go of this anger or annoyance, you are able to listen generously and speak straight far more effectively," Nooyi added.

Best Buy executive chairman Hubert Joly told us, "I may be one of the most naive people on the planet. I've always assumed people are trying their best. Sometimes I get disappointed, but I'm okay with that because I think it's so much more healthy that way than assuming the worst."

The counter to this idea we hear is that sometimes employees really aren't acting in good faith. No question that can be true. Some folks will game the system or count on their boss to be gullible, and some are downright manipulative. We hired a fellow like this once in our corporate days whom we'll call Frank. We quickly realized Frank was one of the most self-absorbed and devious people we'd ever worked with, but because of the benevolent nature of the organization we were working for at the time, it took us years to let him go. By then he had done serious damage to our team's motivation and productivity, not to mention our reputations. We were senior leaders; we were supposed to know better.

Still, with all we went through with Frank, we haven't let it taint our view that it's best to start from the perspective that there's most often an understandable reason for a mistake or underperformance from an employee. And even if a person does have some of Frank's characteristics, we've seen that a good leader's honesty, candidness, and kindness can inspire many of these folks to change.

So, rather than admonishing right away, we encourage leaders to share with employees who confess shortcomings that they are sure they intended to do well. They often discover that the person was quite committed, competent, and on top of the situation, and that unexpected obstacles were put in their way. And even if it turns out that the mistake was that person's fault, it's much better to see it as a chance to teach than an opportunity to punish.

This is a great mind-set to employ to uncover important information about things that go wrong before they get out of hand. Leaders often tell us they learn a lot by slowing down, staying positive, and asking people thoughtful questions about why they think something's gone wrong. After all, if someone has made a mistake, you want them to let you know about it right away. If they're afraid of an explosion or punitive action, they are more likely to try to cover up the problem. As we are wont to say, it's hard to hide a rock under the rug. Pretty soon everyone figuratively stubs their toe or does a face plant into a floor lamp, so isn't it better when problems are shared quickly and we all get to work to fix them?

One example: A leader said she arrived at work one day to find her star employee had up and quit, having left a note of resignation the night before. As the day went on, the leader became more upset. She wasn't just bothered that this employee had left with no notice, but she realized that every person who worked for her had known the guy was going to bolt and had said nothing. Why was she the last to know? In a moment of introspection, she realized her people were not comfortable bringing her bad news. And, to her credit, she knew she had to make some changes as a leader.

Cultures of low trust, where managers react badly to failure, create too negative an environment for productivity and innovation to flow. Creativity requires trust. Who throws out a new idea in a workplace where everyone is focused on self-preservation?

Innovation through Positive Thinking

Former NFL quarterback turned business owner Chad Pennington told us, "In our society, we're teaching our children to avoid failure at all cost. But how do you know what true success is without failing? When you speak with the most successful businessmen and women, they will talk to you about their failures and how they got them where they are. Entrepreneurs (the averages say) fail 3.8 times before they succeed. That's basically one out of four. So we've got to understand there's going to be failure, but we've got to turn it into positive thinking and learning lessons so we can get to the success we desire."

WD-40 Company CEO Garry Ridge agrees. He says, "Around here we don't have mistakes; we have learning moments. A learning moment is a positive or negative outcome of any situation that is openly and freely shared to benefit all. That's why I tell my people that I'm consciously incompetent, because as we embrace learning moments they lead us to the next step and to the next place."

Says Gail Miller, chair of the Larry H. Miller Group of Companies, "You get positive outcomes by being positive and going to work to fix a problem instead of worrying who is to blame. For me, a lot of that mind-set came from growing up poor and knowing whatever I was going to have I had to make happen. My friends would buy their beautiful clothes and I had to go buy fabric and make a skirt. Assuming positive intent is taking a lack and turning it into abundance."

The Four Steps to Stay Composed

We totally get how upsetting, even outright infuriating, it can be to hear that something's been screwed up. When we learn of mistakes made on our team, we are quick to remind ourselves of all the blunders we made coming up and how patient most of our managers were with our errors.

To keep your cool and get the information you need, coach yourself to follow these steps.

First, instead of firing off a rushed text or e-mail, pick up the phone or go see the person (if at all possible)—forcing yourself to speak voice-to-voice to those involved to get to the bottom of the conflict, not to assign blame but to understand the thought process on the issue. Interacting in person or on the phone helps those involved understand your tone is genuine and your reactions are supportive, without the risk of misinterpretation through digital means. Second, take the time necessary to gather all the facts before making any decisions or conclusions. Often your direction will change as you realize your first assumptions weren't correct.

Third, take a forward-looking approach (e.g., instead of asking, "Why did you do that?" you might ask, "What could we do differently in the future when faced with this situation?"). Taking an approach like this to the problem allows you to defuse any existing tension and focus on what we'll do next time to create a positive outcome. And fourth, pay close attention to all communication about the issue to avoid passive-aggressive language and set a positive tone. Another communication factor to consider is your body language during these interactions. You want to avoid giving people the cold shoulder. When we told a friend about this idea, she said this works both ways: "When I was working for a really horrible boss, I got some advice to sit on my hands when I was in a meeting with her, because my body language was giving away how annoyed I was with her. It worked beautifully!"

We saw these ideas in action recently at a client. A talented employee—we'll call her Jasmine—had just been promoted to a coordinator role, and she began to miss deadlines. The executive team discussed how she'd been slipping up, and the quick consensus was that she had been promoted over her abilities and needed to be moved back into the role of an individual contributor. They'd misjudged her talents; lesson learned.

We coached one of the leaders at the executive table, and the advice we'd given about positive intent had really struck him. He asked if he could meet with Jasmine before further action was taken, and in doing so he discovered the problem wasn't as simple as the executive team had assumed. She was so eager to please in her new role that she wasn't turning any projects away, so she'd gotten overwhelmed with assignments. She'd become a dumping ground for multiple big tasks from multiple teams and was getting very little finished. She also didn't have enough organizational knowledge to be able to decide which assignments to prioritize. She was stressed and just as frustrated about the state of affairs as her internal clients were.

What Jasmine needed was for someone to sit down with her and show her how each of the tasks on her plate fit into the organizational strategy and how she should therefore rank them and put them on a realistic timeline. Because her immediate supervisor didn't have that kind of corporate vision himself, the kindly executive volunteered to be Jasmine's mentor. Within a short period of time, she began to flourish again.

She's No Expert Traveler

Many of us have grown up conditioned to assume the negative. And as if a natural negativity bias isn't enough, a few hours of watching network news or a day or two wandering the halls of some workplaces, and even the most optimistic of us can start to believe it's a largely dysfunctional, dog-eat-dog world (and you're wearing Milk-Bone underwear).

That kind of negative perspective is damaging not only to those we manage, but to ourselves, and to all of those we want to be supportive and nurturing of in our personal lives as well.

With so much pressure loaded on us to achieve often unrealistic results at work and so much depressing news in the world, it's important to coach ourselves to regularly look around and make note of the good in people as well as how so many are simply struggling to get by. One leader told a particularly affecting story of such a moment that had a profound effect on her.

Lynn Carnes said that when she was the leader of a risk management group at a bank early in her career, "I was a raging bitch." Carnes, now an executive coach, candidly admitted, "I had an eye for trouble and saw it everywhere I went."

In a discussion with her employees on developing some team core values, her people suggested a value of "assume positive intent." Carnes was unimpressed. Her first thought: "How about a value of 'Do what I say.'" It was with great reluctance that she left the meeting agreeing to try the value out.

"I was assuming negative intent, and I was doing it everywhere," she said. "I was waiting for everyone to make me look bad. It was a self-protective mechanism. If I saw trouble coming, I couldn't let it get me. I did it to be safe, but it wasn't safe."

Then one day in the Denver airport, Carnes rushed into the Expert Traveler line to catch her plane, but as she approached the X-ray machine she came upon a mom with a baby, stroller, and a boatload of bags. Carnes first thought, *This woman is no expert traveler. Why is she in this line?*

"I felt the rage starting to build," Carnes said. "But then she did something that snapped me out of it. She had to put her child on the ground." There, in the middle of a public airport, this harried mother had to place her precious baby where thousands of mucky shoes had walked. Carnes was humbled. "She needed help. I realized she wasn't there to be in my way; she was just trying to get where she was going." So Carnes asked if she could help, and the offer was graciously accepted. Inside this cynical risk manager—so full of self-preservation—a switch was flipped. Carnes's rage evaporated, and it stayed away all day. That moment in the Expert Traveler line was a turning point in her career and life.

No matter the situation you face, you always have a choice, Carnes says. "Once you see that choice, take a pause. In that pause, make up a better story that doesn't make the other person a villain and you a victim."

THERE'S NO WAY around the fact that we are all going to have to deal with mistakes people under our management make. Any of us who are parents are also faced with all sorts of crazy things our kids do that can make us wonder if they've got a brain at all—*Why would you snort M&M's?* Developing a good drill of always assuming the positive is one of the most transformative things we can do to make our own lives more pleasant, in every little way, while also getting the enormous satisfaction of seeing those we lead grow and thrive.

Assume Positive Intent

+ Employee performance is often hampered by a set of factors largely out of their control, such as the lack of proper tools, thorough training, and clear direction—which can be due to changing priorities or confusing explanations from the leader.

+ Leaders who assume positive intent often discover that unexpected obstacles were put in employees' ways. Even if it turns out that someone was at fault, these leaders use mistakes as a chance to teach rather than an opportunity to punish.

+ If employees are afraid of punitive action, they are more likely to try to cover up problems.

+ Cultures of low trust create too negative an environment for productivity and innovation to flourish. Creativity requires trust.

+ Positive intent coaching steps include: 1) Pick up the phone or go see the person (if at all possible); 2) gather all the facts before making any decisions or conclusions; 3) take a forward-looking approach (e.g., "What could we do differently in the future when faced with this situation?"); 4) pay close attention to all communication to avoid passive-aggressive language and set a positive tone.

Chapter 11

Walk in Their Shoes

Let us return to the show *Undercover Boss*. We got a kick out of watching CEOs put on pancake makeup and fake beards so their employees wouldn't spot them. It was comical, as many of their employees wouldn't have recognized their head honchos if they'd worn name badges that said "Hi. I'm your Head Honcho." According to a 2017 survey of one thousand US employees, one-quarter say they wouldn't be able to pick their CEO out of a lineup. As for millennials, 34 percent say they'd fail the test. By the way, if a film crew is following around new trainee "Andy" for no reason, that might be a hint. Just sayin'.

In studying teams of various efficacy, we've never ceased to be amazed by how little many leaders know about the challenges their people are wrestling with in their daily work. In part that's because they've never done their jobs themselves, but it's also because they don't take the time to ask about the difficulties their team members may be encountering.

While many challenges thrown at people are glaringly obvious even to the most aloof managers—the IT system keeps crashing; the new product line is full of glitches—others are much less so (e.g., interpersonal issues with team members, challenges getting information from other departments, new demands raised by customers). Most managers say they feel pretty well informed about the work their people are doing, but when we are able to convince them to take the time to actually sit with their people and observe, or better yet do their employees' jobs alongside them for a while, they tell us they're amazed about the things they discover.

Leaders who develop empathy for others are great enablers of authentic gratitude. While empathy is often seen as a mental exercise—imagining how someone is feeling—we argue the best way to be truly empathetic is to roll up your sleeves and actually walk in their shoes.

That's the principle behind a great leadership program at the California Fairmont Hotel properties we learned of a few years ago. Each year, the company leaders spent a full day working with an employee whose job required them to interact directly with customers. The program was called Walk in Your Shoes. In their days together, the leaders did not just hang out with the property golf pro or taste new menu items. Tom Klein, regional vice president of operations, said, "A few years back I did housekeeping for a day. Executives don the proper uniform, punch in, put away their phones, and follow hotel protocol to the T.

"After spending a day on the housekeeping rotation, I had

a whole new understanding of what it means to do that job. This program really helps us appreciate our colleagues. You also get a very real understanding of how you can make their jobs easier and more efficient."

This practice was not just a show of management trying to make a point that they need to appreciate "'the little people." It was an incredibly eye-opening and paradigm-shifting process that led to a host of great ideas for improving results. It's only by getting to understand what it's like to do a job that a leader can be most effective in assisting people in doing it. That's empathy at its best.

Research from management consulting company DDI has found that empathy is a "critical driver of overall performance" for managers. It has been positively correlated with key management skills including coaching, engaging, and making sound decisions. Yet the researchers found only "40 percent of front-line leaders" were "proficient or strong in empathy."

Of course, we aren't suggesting 60 percent of managers lack a gene associated with the ability to empathize. The pressures of management weigh heavily, and time is tight. Many managers are also far removed from where their people work day-to-day, so they aren't privy to difficult conversations or the discussions team members have every day about the problems they're encountering. They also may not perceive the tension that can course through work areas from time to time. That's why leaders need to get out of their offices, away from their cushy lairs (with their burning incense and

Enya on the headphones), and spend quality time with their people as they are working, and not just in meetings. As they interact with employees in this way, they can observe carefully and ask how things are really going—taking away layers of hierarchy until they are literally face-to-face with employees in their natural habitat. Consider it a corporate safari!

If a leader doesn't have the kind of time to literally step into people's jobs, the good news is there are many other ways to get the insights they need. Coaching yourself to regularly ask people about how they're approaching their work and for them to share some recent accomplishment can bring you into their world in a much more revealing way.

When we discussed this with a small-company CEO we were working with, he told us a story of a great case in point. One of his accounting people rushed into his office right before year end to announce a *Fortune* 10 client was going to pay a large bill well before the typical sixty-day contract agreement, so the company could close its books for the year with that payment made. He immediately started firing off instructions to her about how she should allocate the windfall. Then something dawned on him. He paused, took a breath, and said, "By the way, Mia, it's not lost on me that you must have done some pretty clever convincing to get this client to pay early."

The accountant guffawed and said, "You have no idea." She then proceeded to tell the impressive story of how hard she had worked to submit the invoice into the client's (probably purposefully) complex automated clearinghouse system, and how she then had developed a solid relationship with her contact at the company and had gingerly cajoled the woman into releasing the check ahead of time. Our coachee remarked, "She was so proud to explain what she'd accomplished. And just by pausing and listening, I was able to get this rare glimpse into her world." That gave him a great opportunity to express gratitude to her that was sincere and specific.

So many of the people doing great work are not in the limelight. Some are on the front lines with customers; others are behind the scenes, like this accountant. Often they get little to no recognition from their bosses for their ingenuity and determination.

To get the scoop on the important things they are doing, consider watching them for a while.

You Are Not Spying, You Are Connecting

Garry Ridge, CEO of WD-40 Company, dedicates the first two hours of his day, every day, to being with his people. "I'm out there as they're coming to work, talking to them, asking, 'What's new with you?' Trying to create a real connection is so important that it's something I've done religiously for years."

Sometimes leaders may hang around and watch employees going about their work, which can lead them to notice aspects of excellence they may not have been aware of. These are not only opportunities for gratitude, but the tips learned may also be shared with others around the organization. While doing this, it's crucial that your people don't feel like they're under surveillance. Explain that you're going to be taking some time to observe them because you want to understand better what they are dealing with and how you can be more helpful.

As you work on this observing skill, it's vital to give your undivided attention. When you ask them to share, it's undermining if you get distracted by a text, phone call, or another employee. Take steps to avoid interruptions so you can be fully present. This, of course, is a challenge, as organizations are insanely distracting, especially for those in charge, but you can make every effort to focus during this time and allow interruptions only in emergencies.

For those executives who argue they are too busy for this kind of regular interaction with their people, we present the case of Britt Berrett, who when president of Texas Health Presbyterian Hospital Dallas had every manager in the organization (including himself) leave their offices every day for one hour to connect with their teammates—asking how they could help, if they could remove any barriers to success, and looking for opportunities to express gratitude. Berrett said that dedicated hour of focus on employees brought his staff and management closer together and facilitated real improvements, including a 30 percent increase in employee engagement scores.

Let's Bring Up the Polishers

Part of the process of walking in their shoes is giving public recognition of the work well done that you've spotted, showing respect for the differences people are making. We love a story Eric Schurenberg, president and CEO of *Inc.* magazine, shared with us about how Alan Mulally did this right when he took the helm at Ford.

In his first town hall meeting—tens of thousands of employees watching live and around the globe via satellite—Mulally shared the stage with a beautiful new Ford. The CEO asked the two workers who had vacuumed and polished the vehicle to come up and join him. When they got to the stage, he told them how grateful he was for the care they had taken. Then he led a round of applause for the workers.

Said Schurenberg, "Alan is a very empathetic person, and he is also very aware of the example he sets. This was his first town hall. He wasn't interested in cementing his power with his leadership team, bringing them up and making a show of how the heads of all these Ford lines of business deferred to him. Instead, in front of everyone, he chose to praise the lowest-level people in the room. In addition to being a beautiful gesture to those two guys, it sent a message around the company about how Ford was going to be run. That everyone matters." Much has been written about Mulally's miraculous turnaround of Ford, but few writers have touched on his remarkable ability to use soft skills such as empathy to win the hearts of his people.

Consider, too, Mulally's first meeting with four thousand US dealership operators at Ford Field (where the NFL Lions play). Working without a teleprompter (a first for a Ford CEO), he outlined the plan to save the company and asked the dealers to join the employees as partners in the new way forward—One Ford. "I was thinking, 'Gosh, I've got to demonstrate this is really going to be different, that we're going to love them up,'" Mulally explained to us. So, the new CEO asked all the Ford employees in the room to stand, turn around, and face all four thousand dealers and say, "We love you."

Said Mulally, "They're all looking down at their shoes. They mumbled it. I said, 'Let's try it again.' The second time they had eye contact. For the third time, I said, 'Let's act like we mean it. Smile and tell them you love them. Cuz we do.'"

"That time, the Ford employees boomed out, 'We love you,' and every dealer there knew it was going to be different," Mulally said. "They knew we were in this together and we'd work together to save the company. They were going to be loved up and included and appreciated. It makes my eyes water even now."

Part of that commitment to his dealers included Mulally actually walking in the shoes of dealership employees. As he knows that empathy is not something you can develop and nurture in the safety of your office, he spent time working as a salesperson in a Ford dealership soon after. It's worth emphasizing that better understanding the work of your people may not only reveal ways you could solve problems for them, it might also help you understand ways you can help them improve the customer experience—as Mulally discovered. As his biographer Bryce Hoffman wrote, it only took a few minutes for the new CEO to make his first sale. "In less than an hour, he made two more. Another was pending." Imagine how much the dealers learned from Mulally. Walking in their shoes isn't just about developing empathy; it's also a way to help people improve their performance.

Of course, smart leaders are respectful about how they offer this kind of improvement advice—for instance, asking employees why they're doing things the way they are before correcting them. But as long as leaders are thoughtful in this process, they are typically surprised by how receptive and grateful people can be to constructive critiques that make their work better.

Another leader who worked to develop empathy for his associates from day one was Hubert Joly when he joined Best Buy as CEO. Joly spent his first week not in the corporate offices but working in one of the company's retail stores. "We've got two ears and one mouth, which means we need to do a lot more listening than talking," he told us. "I wanted to learn from our people on the front line, and I learned they were unhappy. For example, the previous leadership team had reduced their employee discount at the same time awarding big retention bonuses to senior executives, so we reinstated the discount. The search engine on the website was not working—they couldn't find products, so we replaced it.

"We took care of our associates' needs first, and that

unleashed unlimited energy and passion because they felt respected and listened to."

Radical Candor

Singularity University founder Rob Nail shared with us another keen insight. He said when you walk in employees' shoes and develop greater empathy for them, they typically are more willing to give you the benefit of the doubt and know you're well intentioned when you give them honest feedback. His organization uses a concept called radical candor to accomplish this.

That term was made popular by Kim Scott, a former Google executive, now cofounder of Candor, LLC. Early in Scott's career at Google, she made a presentation to the big bosses. Her manager, Sheryl Sandberg, gave her some straightforward, unsolicited advice. "Sheryl started the conversation by telling me about the things that had gone well in the meeting. But, of course, all I wanted to hear about was what I had done wrong. Eventually she said, 'You said *um* a lot in there.'"

Scott dismissed her boss's feedback with a wave of her hand, but Sandberg leaned in. "She looked right at me and said, 'I can see when you do that thing with your hand, I'm gonna have to be a lot more direct. When you say *um* every third word, it makes you sound stupid.'"

The interaction "really got me thinking," she said. "What was it about Sheryl that made it so seemingly easy for her to tell me [this], but also why hadn't anybody told me for fifteen years? It was like I'd been walking through my whole career with a hunk of spinach between my teeth and nobody had had the courtesy to tell me it was there."

Rob Nail established the rule at Singularity University that radical candor "has to come with a deep empathy and desire to help the other person. Nothing excuses you being a jerk and giving a lot of stupid feedback. Radical candor is about valuing the other person, being grateful for them, and authentically trying to help them."

He added, "And then, in reverse, as a receiver, you have to make sure you value and thank the person who is giving you feedback. If you know the giver believes in you, wants to help, and has your best interests at heart, then there is real gratitude for their intention. Then something new can happen."

Working Your Empathy Muscles

We know that demonstrating empathy does not come naturally to everyone. If that's true for you, think of this as a form of personal training. You're building up empathy muscle memory. And just as with actual exercise, the benefits will be far-reaching in your life. Getting physically fit improves our mood and boosts confidence, not to mention being good for our overall health. Building empathy strengthens all our relationships in life and makes our daily interactions more rewarding.

The Nature Conservancy CEO Mark Tercek expressed

that he was grateful for advice he received from executive coach Marshall Goldsmith, who told him he needed to work on his empathy skills. "I thought I was doing a good job in many respects in my early days here, but I could tell that on the interpersonal front things were not going as well. It seemed to me like my colleagues were bristling in response to my conversations. It even embarrasses me to say that at times of stress, my dear wife was too."

Goldsmith interviewed many in Tercek's team and reported back: "Mark, you're doing some things well. In other respects, you're really being a jerk." One of the main things Tercek needed to work on was empathetic listening. "I was always cutting people off, trying to show off how smart I was."

Tercek went in front of his team and told them he was going to try to improve in this area. On top of that, he wrote an article about his efforts and published it on LinkedIn, which, he said, was a great way to hold his feet to the fire.

He told us that he had to work at it every day. "It was not as easy as I thought to change those kinds of habits." It took time, but he's found positive effects in every aspect of his life. "In this job I go to events and schmooze, and that started to be more fun for me because I was paying more attention to what people were saying. I was just being a more decent person." Perhaps most rewarding has been the response from his family. "One day, my daughter says, 'Dad, what happened? You're being so nice!'" Tercek laughs now. "That's sort of what they call a left-handed compliment. But it was the truth."

A few ideas to get the stories rolling are to put together a list of conversation starters when you are with your employees, such as:

- Who are you working with in the company and what have you learned from them lately?
- What's been your best day at work in the last few weeks (and why)?
- What's up with your family?
- Where have you gone on vacation recently?
- What are you most proud of at work?
- How would you describe our culture to new employees (what's good, what's not so great)?
- How do you think we do working across team boundaries?
- As you look back at your last week, what would you have done differently?
- What's fun about working here?

Walk in Their Shoes

+ Many leaders know very little about the challenges their people wrestle with in their daily work. They don't take the time to ask about difficulties their team members may be encountering.

+ One of the great enablers of authentic gratitude is developing empathy for others. The best way to be truly empathetic is to actually walk in their shoes. One way leaders can bring themselves into employees' worlds in a much more revealing way is by coaching themselves to regularly ask people about how they're approaching their work and if they could share some recent accomplishments.

+ Better understanding the work of their people may not only reveal ways leaders could help solve problems for them, it might also help them understand how they can help workers improve the customer experience and their overall performance.

+ Radical candor has to come with a deep empathy and desire to help others. In reverse, receivers have to make sure they value and thank the person who is giving them feedback and know they have their best interests at heart.

Chapter 12

Look for Small Wins

At Connecticut-based nonprofit Ability Beyond, staff members help people with disabilities lead fuller, more rewarding lives. It can be a thankless job. "Our direct care staff sometimes help people in every aspect—bathing, feeding, and dressing. That can become normal routine, and gratitude just isn't part of the picture," president and CEO Jane Davis shared with us. "We have tried employee appreciation days, nurses' week, and so on, but I think most impactful is very specific gratitude for a job well done when you see it."

On the day we spoke with Davis, she told us about a recent experience. "I noticed out the window a person we serve who happens to be on the autism spectrum and was having a really tough morning—like we all do! Although I could not hear what was happening, I could see the staff member working with him was being patient and kind. The conversation ended with a hug. Seeing that prompted a note to thank the employee for that moment and share with him how beautiful it was to watch. It's easy to forget the impact of your work day-to-day, but it makes such a difference."

What a simple moment Davis noticed—one that happens dozens of times a day at an organization like Ability Beyond—and yet every small step in the service of a team's goals and values is worthy of acknowledgment. The ongoing, cumulative effect of small outcomes can be huge.

When we talked about this idea with former NFL quarterback Chad Pennington, who now runs a charity, coaches a high school football team, and is a successful stock contractor (providing animals for rodeos), he heartily agreed about the importance of valuing small, daily successes. He told us, "The only way you get to big wins and big goals is to accomplish your little goals and little wins—that's why celebrating those is really important."

Pennington recalled his days as a college football player at Marshall University, when he had to run every step up the mammoth Joan C. Edwards Stadium. "I had to hit every step. If you skip a few steps, you're gonna bust your shins up and be hurt. Celebrating small wins gives people the motivation to move on to the next one, and it gives a short period of reflection to see where you've come from and where you need to go. It also helps you to be grateful for the people who have entered your life to help."

Harvard Business School professor Teresa Amabile and writer Steven Kramer conducted extensive research on creative breakthroughs in organizations. They found: "Of all the things that can boost emotions, motivation, and perceptions during a workday, the single most important is making progress in meaningful work. And the more frequently people experience that sense of progress, the more likely they are to be creatively productive in the long run. Whether they are trying to solve a major scientific mystery or simply produce a high-quality product or service, everyday progress—even a small win—can make all the difference in how they feel and perform."

For all of us, this indicates that managers have more influence over the engagement, happiness, and creative output of employees than they may realize—and expressing regular gratitude for incremental progress is key.

Former Ford chief Alan Mulally explained to us that rewarding small wins shows a leader knows what's going on. In his weekly business plan review, each member of his leadership team was expected to present a color-coded update of his or her progress toward meeting key company goals. Projects that were on track or ahead of schedule were green, yellow indicated the initiative had issues, and red signaled a program that was behind schedule or off plan.

"The whole thing is really based on gratitude," he said. "When someone shows a red, we say, 'Thank you for that visibility.' When we work a red to a yellow, we thank everybody. Celebrations for each step show the team that it's expected behavior to make progress. When we move from yellow to green, there's another celebration. People are feeling 'Wow. I'm needed. I'm supported.' Gratitude is part of having fun, enjoying the journey and each other."

Signposts to Success

Retired American Express chairman Ken Chenault told us, "The way I look at the little pats on the back: They're signposts for how you're doing. If I'm on a journey, I've got to look for signs that I'm going in the right direction. Points of recognition are those signposts that enable me to complete the journey.

"I think sometimes people get confused. If a leader waits until the big event, I (as an employee) may never get there. I may not have the confidence. I may not have the encouragement that this is a journey worth completing." Well said.

Singularity University founder and CEO Rob Nail told us a great story about the remarkable uplift that can be generated from expressions of gratitude for the small things that happen in a workplace on a regular basis. "Someone in our office kept leaving notes on my desk, almost every week. Things like, 'Wow, that was amazing what you just did at that meeting.'" Nail was profoundly touched and determined to find the anonymous source of this gratitude.

Eventually he solved the mystery and asked the employee about the practice. "She said she journaled every day about one hundred things she was grateful for. Each day she started the list again with a blank page." From that practice, this woman got inspiration for notes not only for Nail but the others she worked with. The result was a team that felt lifted because someone was paying attention to the above-and-beyond things they were doing every single day.

Imagine the lift to morale and productivity in most workplaces if that kind of gratitude came routinely from not only peers but their leaders. One of the most distinctive attributes we've seen in great executives—aside from better hair than us—is that they notice and express appreciation for small-scale efforts as much as they celebrate major achievements. They look for incremental wins every day that they can acknowledge. This allows them to find ways to inspire all their people to stretch and grow. When managers get starstruck and focus only on their best performers and the most substantial victories, they overlook the vital contributions of people we like to call the Steady Eddys (though we also considered Stable Mabels, Constant Connies, and Reliable Rauls).

Now, this is not to say that managers shouldn't be vigilant about expressing gratitude to their stars. It's crucial to identify one's top performers and let them know you understand the difference they're making. Managers who are afraid to single out outstanding achievements by their high-fliers neglect those people at their peril. When high-impact performers are asked why they left an organization, many report: "No one ever asked me to stay!"

But with that said, we cannot emphasize enough how important it is to appreciate your Steady Eddys, those who show up every day to do the often unacclaimed, low-prestige work that keeps the doors open and customers satisfied. They are the backbone of businesses, and they need encouragement too. Managers too often underestimate the importance of even brief gratitude for tasks that may be overlooked. We've seen some especially impressive ways in which managers are doing this.

Great Ways to Spot Small Wins

By their humble nature, small wins can be hard to detect. So we've compiled here our favorite set of simple ways to elicit the help of others in spotting them:

Ask team members to give shout-outs to each other.
At SnackNation in Culver City, California, every Friday afternoon the leadership asks the entire one hundred–person team to come together. Employees take a few moments to recognize another team member they're grateful for, explaining how that person helped them during the week. Not only does this provide gratitude to workers who normally might not get a lot of the spotlight, but it has a terrific residual effect: Employees are educated weekly about the projects that other departments are working on. That not only facilitates better understanding of the wider range of the company's operations but encourages crossing of team lines and building of social connections between departments. Breaking down silos in this way increases trust, communication, and the agility of the entire organization—not to mention that it helps create a one-company mentality and makes Friday afternoons less of a drag and more of a party. One study showed 70 percent of customer service professionals and executives

believe a "silo mentality" is the biggest obstacle to effectively serving their customers.

Ask team members to toot their own horns.

One manager we met devised another great way to get employees to inform him of small successes. He asked them to write up and e-mail him quick case studies of their own wins. The results were one- or two-page (max) summaries in which the employee described the problem faced, what steps she took to resolve it (the action), who else was involved (the team), and the results achieved. The employee then got to take five minutes in the next staff meeting to explain the win and, most important, what she learned from the experience and if there was anything she might do differently if faced with the same situation. The employee was expected to be grateful to those who helped her, and the manager then would take a moment to express gratitude for the win himself. He told us this has really boosted the engagement of his team, and, if you think about it, how easy is this for that leader? The employees literally do everything from soup to nuts, and all he has to do is add a few words at the end, smile, and reap the benefits. Brilliant.

Ameet Mallik, executive vice president and head of US Novartis Oncology, said that in his weekly Friday touch point meetings with his leadership team, he has begun asking each participant to share something that happened during the week they are proud of, that they are grateful for. "It sets a tone for the rest of the call. It takes ten minutes for everyone to contribute, and it is a very powerful way of insti-tutionalizing gratitude and positivity." Pretty soft stuff for a left-brained executive who finished in the top 5 percent of his Wharton MBA class and has an advanced degree in bio-technology from Northwestern, but Mallik is a remarkable executive who understands how to implement a "we" versus "me" mind-set in his team.

Set and then reward achievement of daily, weekly, or thirty-day goals.

Instead of only focusing their thanks for the attainment of big goals, great leaders set shorter targets and express grati-tude for all the mini milestones achieved. One company that has mined for such goodwill is retailer TJX Canada (which operates brands such as Marshalls, Winners, and Home-sense). When we were asked to speak at their annual confer-ence, we were thrilled that each of the managers was given a little gold miner's burlap bag with a collection of tokens inside to use as rewards for employees who hit incremental goals. On the front of the token was the TJX logo, and on the back the words "A token of appreciation for being amaz-ing. Thank you." A simple idea and a powerful way for man-agers to keep momentum rolling in their stores.

Spotlight those who speak up and offer ideas.

Inc. writer Drew Gannon tells the story of video game com-pany Frima Studio, which encourages employees to pres-ent potential project ideas. When narrative designer David

Moss was hired, he put together a team on his own to pitch a mythological adventure for young boys set in fourteenth-century Scotland. The twist—instead of a video game, the team thought it would be best as an animated TV show, which was well outside the company's expertise. The team presented its idea to a jury of peers, and "by the end of the presentation, everyone's eyes lit up and they could see the potential," Moss said. The jury decided it was a smart idea, and Frima's upper management agreed, rewarding Moss and the team with full funding and time to work on the exciting project.

Smart leaders understand they must foster and reward employee ideas if they want to continue to grow, and that means creativity must be acknowledged and rewarded, all of which brings more ideas and innovation to the table.

Recognize those who find new productivity hacks.
One manager told us he had just rewarded an employee after learning of this simple productivity hack: The employee spent the last five minutes of his day putting together to-dos for his next day. Said the employee, "I was wasting a bunch of time every morning going over what I'd worked on the day before and figuring out where I needed to pick up on again. By planning my next day before I head out at night, I can hit the ground running the minute I get to work." It was a humble hack—it probably only saved ten minutes or so each morning—but when the manager rewarded the worker publicly, he spread that idea to the entire team. Soon

everyone was doing it, and productivity improved by hours every day.

Thank those who find solutions to resolve conflicts.
Getting along is a key to workplace success, and managers who value emotional intelligence in their team members are rewarding an unsung skill. Smart managers thank employees when they are more inclusive, and they train them to be more mindful of how their words and actions may unintentionally offend others—helping reduce instances of workplace bullying. Gratitude is part of the tool kit when smart leaders intervene in positive ways to encourage employees to treat their coworkers as partners in the team, reduce bickering, and move past emotional struggles they are having with each other.

Make great use of anniversaries.
Jonathan Klein, chairman of Getty Images, told us employees' key work anniversaries are a great opportunity to catch up on all the thank-yous that may have been missed along the way. As such, he personally writes a thank-you note to each of his two thousand employees on their big career milestones to show gratitude and appreciation.

Klein has also made a great point that leaders should spread small expressions of gratitude widely—to customers, suppliers, and even with people they hope might one day join their team. He told a story of bringing a new employee on board because of an expression of gratitude. "We were very keen to hire somebody from a competitor. He spent ages considering whether to leave his previous 'home,' where his father had worked throughout his career. He finally decided not to join. I called him to thank him for considering and to express that I completely understood his decision. I also sent him a note."

A year later, that talented employee called to say he was now ready to make the move to Getty. "He stressed how influential that call and expression of gratitude was to him and his subsequent decision to join us," said Klein.

Said the chairman, "I recognized very early on that the resources we have as leaders are finite. It also struck me that there is one resource that is infinite and makes a huge difference. That is gratitude. It will never run out, costs nothing, and has a major impact."

Seeing Becomes a Better Way of Being

Once you're using some of these ways to get the scoop on small wins and you are seeing the effects of your gratitude, we hope you will naturally find yourself looking for them more often. To not lose sight of small wins, we encourage leaders to keep a work gratitude journal—electronically or in a small notebook—that they keep with them at all times. That way they can write brief observations of jobs well done as soon they see them and consult it regularly to send out their thank-yous to team members.

Ken Chenault took the *charge* of gratitude seriously when

he led American Express. He would observe thankable behaviors and either call the individual soon after or send an e-mail of thanks when he got back to his office. It was all about giving credit right away. "I would tell them that they made a very meaningful difference, they gave me an insight," he said. "I tried to make the feedback as immediate as possible so they understood that the impact was important to me."

Let's just say this about Chenault's gratitude journal: He never left home without it. Thank you. Thanks so much. Please, keep your seats.

This kind of immediacy is a great way to appreciate how people's contributions far outweigh any challenges they are facing (or even mistakes they've made) and keep a leader's assessment of their work in a constructive perspective. The practice of small-win spotting also can have great spillover effects in the rest of a leader's life. Disruption and innovation author Whitney Johnson emphasized to us that paying attention to little wins in our lives can help us through difficult times.

The year 2012, she said, brought many successes in her professional career, and yet it also was a year of heartache. "My brother took his life, my husband was diagnosed with cancer, and we had huge financial setbacks."

As she struggled with these challenges, Johnson read a news article about a group of teenagers who had been hiking in the Arizona desert. One was bitten by a rattlesnake. Instead of rushing the affected teen to the emergency room, the group spent hours chasing down the snake to kill it.

By the time the teens returned to their stricken friend, the venom had spread and doctors eventually had to amputate the friend's limb.

"That stayed with me in a really powerful way," she said. "When we are hurt, we have to decide are we going to go after the person who hurt us, or are we going to get the venom out of our system? I could have been bitter that things weren't going the way I wanted, but that venom of bitterness could have killed me."

"That's when I had the epiphany of gratitude. Every day I would look for things I was grateful for, basic things: 'I'm grateful for my family, for my husband, for my children,' or 'Today I'm grateful for clean water or for modern medicine.' It took being in this moment of absolute depths to understand the only way through was to find the small things I was grateful for, every day."

It's not uncommon in our world for people to adopt an attitude of *I'll be grateful when* . . . They believe happiness will come when they get that new job or earn more money or finish school or retire or their thirty-five-year-old children move out, and then they will be grateful. But as we've asked the leaders in this book to recall the time in their careers when they grew the most, when they felt the most grateful, it was during the hardest of times. To a person they choose to focus on the small blessings to get them through.

One story we were particularly affected by was from Mark Cole, CEO of the John Maxwell Companies. He said, "I was a preacher's kid. Small church of 250 people. So literally people giving into the Sunday offering put food on our table. I grew up realizing what I have is because of the generosity of others. That created a profound gratitude every day."

When he was about thirty years old, Cole told us he made a career transition and "it was a difficult time financially. To make ends meet, I washed trucks in the middle of the night. For months I was in such a desperate situation that I would buy a bag of potato chips and would count how many chips were in the bag so that it would last me the entire week. I know, grab the Kleenexes."

Cole is forever grateful to John Maxwell, who took a chance on him and helped secure his financial future. But that tough time changed him for the better. "Just last night my grandson wanted chips. I pulled out the bag and said, 'Hey, Ryder, let's count how many there are.' I told him about the time G-Pa only had one bag of potato chips to last all week. I want him to know that everything we have today comes from a place where there was nothing. That keeps my gratitude going."

Look for Small Wins

- Every small step toward an organization's goals and values is worthy of acknowledgment. The ongoing, cumulative effect of small outcomes can be significant.
- Research finds the single most important factor in boosting motivation in the creative process is when employees feel they are making daily progress in meaningful work.
- One of the most distinctive attributes of great leaders is they notice and express appreciation for small-scale efforts as much as they celebrate major achievements. This allows them to find ways to inspire all their people to stretch and grow, including the steady performers in their care.
- Good leaders also identify top performers and let them know they understand the difference they're making. When high-impact performers are asked why they left an organization, many report: "No one ever asked me to stay!"
- Some of the best ways to spot small wins include: Ask team members to give shout-outs to each other; ask employees to communicate their own wins; set and then reward achievement of daily, weekly, or thirty-day goals (instead of just major accomplishments); spotlight those who speak up and offer ideas; recognize new productivity hacks; thank those who find solutions to resolve potential conflicts with coworkers; and make great use of anniversaries.

Expressing

Chapter 13

Give It Now, Give It Often, Don't Be Afraid

Like ripe bananas, gratitude does not keep. The closer to an achievement a leader expresses her appreciation, the better.

Too many leaders figure they'll stockpile their praise and share it all at once, maybe in a quarterly one-on-one, or even all the way at the end of the year in a performance review. We've found that many managers think they'll remember the positive stuff but usually don't. Many also tell us the best gauge of a person's contributions is the reports they get that offer up quantitative measures—gross sales, units produced, deliveries made without breakage, number of employment candidates placed, or other KPIs. After all, they explain, their people can *look* like they're doing great work, but at the end of the day, if they're not getting the results, why should their behavior be praised? It's true we've probably all known or managed an employee who sure looked busy and yet just didn't ever seem to get much done, at least not at the quality or quantity necessary.

Some managers have also told us that they believe discussing accomplishments during performance reviews is a more formal, and therefore more meaningful, approach to gratitude. Performance appraisals can certainly be effective, providing valuable evidence-based assessments of employee results, as well as setting concrete individual development goals. We're not saying managers should forgo quantitative assessments of output; we believe this can be hugely informative, especially for the employees involved who are often unaware about issues in their performance. The information can also be a vital tool for managers in helping them coach their people to figure out what needs to change and to lead them to improved results. All good.

But a note of caution is called for. One much-discussed problem with the annual review is that sometimes it is overly weighted toward criticism and can feel punitive to the employee. Even well-intended reviews can cause intense employee resentment if they are not tempered by frequent positive reinforcement throughout the rest of the year.

Let's assume a manager is thoughtful, makes constructive criticism, and even offers some well-deserved praise in a review of quantitative performance. Even so, many important *qualitative* contributions, which can't be directly tied to a number, are often lost in the quantitative weeds. When only graded on sales, employees are more likely to avoid mentoring younger workers, for instance. When graded solely on individual productivity, helping others can be shelved.

The infrequent formal feedback process leaves so many day-to-day achievements unacknowledged. That wastes golden opportunities to provide immediate positive reinforcement of the behaviors a leader is looking for, day in and day out. It also wastes chances to lift employees out of the frustration they may be feeling about their challenges, which can be a real productivity killer.

The Path to Progress Is a Bumpy Road

We return to the findings of Harvard researcher Teresa Amabile and writer Steven Kramer, which we introduced in the last chapter. Their work has focused on getting inside the minds of employees and understanding what motivates them, which they reported in the *Harvard Business Review*. Recall they uncovered extraordinary evidence of the effects of feeling we've made progress during a day on our overall motivation. The study was conducted with the members of twenty-six project teams who were assigned to all sorts of different projects—from IT work to creating new kitchen products. Team members were asked to write a diary entry at the end of every workday for the duration of the project, typically about four months.

When Amabile and Kramer analyzed the entries, they found that having made some amount of progress in a day correlated with people feeling good about their work and being strongly motivated to continue. On the flip side, if people hadn't made progress during a work shift or had experienced a setback, they were more likely to be strongly deflated and their intrinsic motivation took a real hit.

This may not seem earth-shattering, but a couple of key aspects of their findings are especially relevant. One is that people got a big lift even from having made what might seem like small steps forward. One employee diary entry said: "I smashed that (computer) bug that's been frustrating me for almost a calendar week. That may not be an event to you, but I live a very drab life, so I'm all hyped." Another learning is that even small setbacks can be damaging to energy and morale, and the effects are disproportionately more powerful than those of making progress. This research vividly portrays what an emotional roller-coaster ride work can be day-in and day-out for most team members, which can have big effects on performance.

By frequently checking in with people and helping them see they've made appreciable progress each day, leaders can boost energy levels considerably. Even more important, this study shows how hard people can be on themselves about a perceived lack of progress. Frequent gratitude gives team members perspective that setbacks aren't the end of the world and can point out achievements—even small ones— they may have overlooked.

We've heard too many managers say that they reserve their praise for when the job gets done. But even a modicum of gratitude on a regular basis is helpful in getting people recharged.

The Mind Is Designed for Regular Feedback

Timeliness of gratitude communicates that a leader is paying attention, and that giving credit when it's due is a priority in his busy world. A lack of timeliness? That can get under the skin fast. Just try missing your spouse's birthday by a day; it can be difficult to get a good night's sleep on the La-Z-Boy. Never underestimate how potent a perceived gratitude slight may be. We talked with one employee who still harbored resentment from years before, when his boss had failed to thank him for considerable overtime he'd put in on a network upgrade. If you can recall irritation for not receiving appreciation from a boss at some point in your career, you are not alone. When we ask people to recount such experiences, their responses usually come tumbling out.

The other big issue with delaying expressions of gratitude is that it prevents effective positive reinforcement. While we know that rewarded behavior gets repeated, we may not be as aware that the science of positive reinforcement shows that the effects are much more powerful when rewards are offered in close proximity to acts.

When we've raised this point with managers, some of them respond that their people are adults, not kids who need training to clean up their rooms or brush their teeth. They also aren't puppies, as one fellow said to us, "who you have to catch in the act of peeing on the rug or they won't learn." Um, true, we guess. The problem is, these managers are underestimating the deep psychological mechanisms of positive reinforcement, which are built into us and stay with us through our entire lives, and can be an exceptional leadership tool in the box.

Consider a remarkable study that sought to measure the effects of positive reinforcement on getting hospital staff to wash their hands more frequently. Despite voluminous research showing that hand washing has a huge effect on lowering transmission of disease in hospitals, it's still not done nearly enough. Tali Sharot, a professor of cognitive neuroscience at University College London, writes about research conducted at a New York state hospital to combat the problem. As in most hospitals, this one had lots of warning signs about the results of unsanitized hands. There were enough sanitization gel dispensers around the place to fill a swimming pool. Yet cameras that monitored every sink and hand sanitizer in the hospital's intensive care unit revealed that only 10 percent of staff cleaned their hands before and after entering a patient's room. Employees knew they were being recorded, but that didn't change anything.

The hospital administrators then put an electronic board in the hallway, giving employees instant feedback on their efforts. With each instance of an employee washing his or her hands, the board displayed a positive message about the activity— e.g., "Thanks for staying clean for our patients!"—and the current shift's hand-hygiene score went up. Compliance rates reached almost 90 percent within four weeks. Says Sharot, "Why did this intervention work so well? Instead of using the threat of spreading disease, the common approach in this situation, the researchers chose a positive strategy. Every time a staff member washed their hands, they received immediate *positive* feedback. Positive feedback triggers a reward signal in the brain, reinforcing the action that caused it, and making it more likely to be repeated in the future."

How Often Is Often Enough?

Surveys from Gallup show members of the most engaged teams report feeling some form of acknowledgment of their contributions from their leader or fellow teammates about once every seven days. If you don't have your calculator with you, that's thirty-five times a year for each person you manage, or about once every week to two. If you have the typical five to fifteen people working directly under your purview, we hope you might find ways to give each of them some modicum of positive reinforcement with that frequency. Now, if you manage a larger team, say of a hundred, we feel your pain. If you were to try to make time to show gratitude to each person every week, you'd be running around the office like a glad-handing politician on a whistle-stop campaign tour. And honestly, no one would welcome your drive-by thanks.

The good news is that even with large teams, there are many ways to ensure people receive frequent expressions of appreciation for jobs well done, if not from you, then from their immediate colleagues. Key for a leader is to set the pace and explicitly ask everyone on the team to help out. For direct reports, leaders can ask them to make this a mission, and of course to practice with them what they're preaching. It's amazing how often we visit with a CEO or divisional leader who expresses deep-seated commitment to this practice of gratitude, and then soon after the head of HR (or another executive) will take us aside and say, "Uh, yeah. He may say that, but he doesn't get this stuff at all. We need you to get through to him."

When we share the Gallup data on frequency, some leaders tell us they worry about giving people too much praise. Let us settle the score on that. In all of our years of coaching leaders, we have yet to encounter that problem. Having sent out surveys to hundreds of thousands of employees asking them what's good and bad about the way they're being managed, we have never once seen the complaint "My boss thanks me way too much. I can't get anything done around here what with all the adulation!" Just ask yourself: How many colleagues have you heard lamenting the overabundance of gratitude they are struggling with? Anyone?

In short, don't be a gratitude tightwad.

Be Not Afraid

In earlier chapters we've provided various ways to identify specific achievements, big and small, and how to express gratitude for them. And yet many leaders are still afraid to give it a shot. Certainly we have seen a few blunders, beyond just offering the bland platitudes we've covered. We actually overheard one manager tell an employee, "I wanted to tell you that Beth said yesterday how much she's enjoyed working with you. That was great to hear because I've had so many complaints from others." Oh, so close.

Charles Schwab, founder of Charles Schwab Corporation, reminds us all that moments of gratitude should always include positive words, never negative. Schwab once said, "I consider my ability to arouse enthusiasm among my people the greatest asset I possess, and the way to develop the best that is in a person is by appreciation and encouragement. There is nothing that kills the ambitions of a person more than criticism from superiors. I never criticize anyone. I am hearty in my appreciation and lavish in my praise."

As Schwab suggests, the gratitude of a leader can be undermined with negative words. Before anything is said, ask yourself: Is it kind, is it true, is it necessary? (A thought often attributed to Buddha as well as many others, but the original source is anonymous.)

Using positive language may seem like officious advice, but we have seen leaders go off script too often, to detrimental effect. While a leader may have had to step in and help with a situation or project to make it a success, an expression of gratitude isn't about the manager, and leadership isn't about keeping score. We recommend keeping that part to themselves. And while some employees may have come a long way and learned hard-knock lessons in the pursuit of ultimate success, a gratitude moment isn't the time or place for a leader to remind anyone of early failures. Expressions of gratitude are times to celebrate and make your people feel valued and rewarded.

And so, there is no good reason to fear. As we close this chapter, let us put to rest a few last worries we hear from managers about their expressions of gratitude.

Jealousy: "If I say thanks to one person, I'm going to have the rest of my team ticked off at me," leaders fear. But when they are frequent in their gratitude, and when thanks are specifically aligned with core values, this jealousy problem typically disappears. *You know, he's right: Gwendolyn really does deserve the credit.* It's when gratitude is rare that the "employee of the month/year" is too often resented.

Triteness: "Gratitude won't mean as much if it's too frequent," say some leaders. To counter that, imagine you go to a child's soccer game and decide, as a group of parents and supporters, that all the clapping and cheering is really too much (and chafing your hands), so you are going to hold your applause until the end of the game . . . *if* they win. Ridiculous, right? And yet how often do leaders take this approach? Gratitude doesn't get old if it's aligned with what the leader and the team value most (nor do halftime orange slices).

Inconsistency: "It's too easy to miss stuff my people are doing," some managers tell us. As any referee or line judge can attest, no one can spot everything. That's why many of the leaders we've studied ask their team members to help them identify things to celebrate every day—picking up actions they wouldn't normally catch on their own.

Uncertainty: "I wouldn't want to guess what my people would like as a reward," say some apprehensive bosses. These folks are paralyzed by trying to weigh what to give their people that would be meaningful and memorable.

As it happens, that's exactly where we are going next.

Give It Now, Give It Often, Don't be Afraid

- Some leaders think they'll stockpile their praise and share it during performance reviews, but many important contributions and day-to-day achievements are lost by then.

- A reliance on the performance review as a primary means of providing feedback wastes golden opportunities to offer immediate reinforcement of the exact behaviors a leader is looking for.

- By checking in with people and helping them see they've made appreciable progress each day, leaders can boost energy levels considerably. Frequent gratitude also gives team members perspective that setbacks aren't the end of the world and can point out achievements—even small ones—they may have overlooked.

- Rewarded behavior gets repeated. Delaying expressions of gratitude prevents effective positive reinforcement. Positive reinforcement triggers a reward signal in the brain that reinforces the action and makes it more likely to be repeated in the future.

- Data shows members of the most engaged teams report feeling acknowledgment of their contributions from their leader or fellow teammates about once every seven days.

Chapter 14

Tailor to the Individual

Our friend Kent is a director of learning and development in the software industry. He told us a terrific story about the need to tailor gratitude to the individual. After working for months on a new employee orientation program, he introduced a method that would allow the company to bring new hires up to speed in half the time of the old way of doing things. The first-year estimated savings to the company was in excess of seventy-five thousand dollars. Kent was understandably proud of his achievement. He was not surprised when, at the next staff meeting, one of the company leaders presented him with a gift card for his hard work.

"I thought, okay, that's nice, a twenty-five-dollar gift card," he told us. "I probably wouldn't have thought that much about it except for what happened next."

The senior executive who had recognized Kent clapped her hands and said, "Now, let's have some fun. Who can name the teams in this weekend's Super Bowl?" The woman sitting next to Kent raised her hand and got the question right. Her prize? You guessed it: Exact. Same. Twenty-five-dollar gift card.

Our friend laughed when he told us the story. "I wasn't upset, I thought it was funny. But I also didn't leave feeling my work was that appreciated."

More than seventy-five thousand people have now taken our Motivators Assessment, and the results have highlighted that each person on this planet has a unique combination of what drives him/her on the job. To build the assessment, we worked with Drs. Travis Bradberry and Jean Greaves, authors of the book *Emotional Intelligence 2.0* and founders of the intelligence assessment company TalentSmart. These eminent psychologists and their team of behavioral scientists tested potential motivators on working adults from around the world to determine which are the most common and significant. What emerged was a final set of twenty-three workplace motivators.

Autonomy
Challenge
Creativity
Developing others
Empathy
Excelling
Excitement
Family
Friendship
Fun
Impact

Learning
Money
Ownership
Pressure
Prestige
Problem solving
Purpose
Recognition
Service
Social responsibility
Teamwork
Variety

Our results showed all humans share this group of fundamental motivators at work. The nuances in a person's specific nature show up not only in which of these are most important to him or her, but also in the particular order of priority—from one to twenty-three.

As we've shared these motivators with leaders, they've had some epiphanies. For example, we visited a large medical center suffering from high turnover in its nursing ranks. Valuable CNAs, LPNs, and RNs were walking out the door almost as fast as the organization could hire them. The seniormost leader said, "I believe we have been missing the mark with our nurses. What motivates a labor-and-delivery nurse is vastly different from what motivates an emergency room nurse or an oncology nurse. But we've been treating them all the same—they have all been 'nurses' to us. We need to start understanding what really motivates someone joining a particular team, or even someone who's been here for a long time. We need to put people in the right roles, for sure, but we also need to give each nurse specific assignments they'll find motivating and rewarding."

Exactly. Some people working in the same jobs might be especially jazzed by collaborating with a team, while others are more driven to learn something new by themselves, and yet others want to help their colleagues develop their own talents. Some are driven strongly by the desire to make a lot of money, while others care more about being able to exercise their creativity.

Smart leaders use that knowledge of individual motivators to tailor expressions of gratitude to each team member. For instance, someone driven by concepts such as autonomy and excelling might feel best recognized when given a chance to work independently on an important project, while someone who is more motivated by concepts such as teamwork and friendship would likely feel more valued when thrown a party with work friends in celebration of a big win.

Said former NFL quarterback Chad Pennington, "Tailoring your gratitude toward the specific individual shows first, empathy, and second, that you are in tune to what he or she is accomplishing. It shows they specifically matter to the success of the team."

"There's no 'I' in team, but there is an 'm' and an 'e,'" he added. "Sometimes people can hide behind the concept of team and not put forth the individual effort to make the group better. So, when a leader actually acknowledges with gratitude that's targeted to an individual who is excelling, that uplifts the person who's making the team better."

We spoke about this idea with Jane Martínez Dowling, president and CEO of ExpandED Schools, a nonprofit that creates after-school programs for more than one million children in New York City. She says individualizing gratitude is essential as she works with her staff and the young people they serve—especially girls and people of color who can feel marginalized by society. "I come from a culture where it's important to say how you feel every day," she said. "Gratitude is interwoven into everything I do and has to be based on the person receiving it—from how I sign e-mails, to how I begin and end sentences, to how I celebrate their milestones. A smile might exude gratitude to one person, where sometimes gratitude is a text or note to an individual that lets them know I am thinking about them, and that I know they're doing the best they can."

The Gray Area of Gratitude

Unfortunately, too often managers look through their own lenses when expressing gratitude and therefore see things only in a way that is comfortable and familiar to them. Our brains don't like gray areas. Think about it this way: In the run-up to an election, if we like a certain candidate, we have a tendency to see nothing but sunshine and unicorns about our guy and nothing but faults about his competitors. And what happens, for instance, if our white-hat candidate makes a statement on camera that is, um, off-brand? We tend to dismiss it. Our guy is good; he couldn't say something that is bad. We crave black and white.

But life is rarely simple; gratitude most certainly is not. Not everyone in our care appreciates the same rewards, and they often value very different things from their leaders. The two of us learned this lesson early in our careers, and it would go on to help shape some of our later research.

Almost twenty years ago now, when we first met, we worked together as young, fresh-faced leaders in a large corporation. At the time, Chester asked his CEO if he would reward Adrian for a big achievement: writing and publishing the company's first leadership book. As background, some of Chester's top motivators are friendship, fun, and teamwork, so he figured he knew just how Adrian would like to be appreciated—exactly how he himself would like to be. Chester asked the CEO to invite Adrian to an evening black-tie gala with the entire sales team (who Adrian didn't work with and didn't really know), and he would be presented with a nice watch at the end of the night. What a great time Adrian would have, Chester mused, making wonderful new friends from around the country. And the watch would be perfect because Chester loves watches and he noticed Adrian didn't wear one.

Now, understand that Adrian's top three motivators are creativity, family, and autonomy. For him, the motivators of fun, friendship, and teamwork (so important to Chester) rank sixteenth, nineteenth, and twenty-first respectively out of twenty-three. While he's not a complete misanthrope, socializing isn't what gets Adrian jazzed about working. If back then Chester had an understanding of his friend's motivators, he might have asked the CEO to reward him with a chance to lead a new innovation, or perhaps time off to be with his loved ones. Unfortunately, Chester had no clue back then. So while Adrian certainly appreciated the effort—he knew in his heart they all meant well—the reward wasn't as meaningful as it could have been as he spent a work night away from his family in a room full of people he didn't know to receive a wristwatch that's still in the box two decades later.

While we tell that story as an example of recognition that could have been more targeted, a vital lesson we also learned is to be thankful for all sincere gratitude that comes our way. Adrian was gracious in this case, as he should have been, and when we address employee groups we stress that all praise and compliments from your leaders really should be appreciated, that it pays to be diplomatic, even if an award misses the mark, and to be accepting of people who tell us we are excelling.

When we were children, we used to love being cheered and complimented. As adults, too, many people downplay their accomplishments and shoo away compliments. They hear, "Nice work on that proposal," to which they reply, "Oh, that wasn't my best work." Or when someone says, "That blouse looks wonderful on you," they fire back, "It would if I hadn't gained all this weight."

Please remember that "thank you" is the perfect reply to gratitude; in fact, it's the only one necessary. When we are ungrateful for gratitude, it lessens the gift, insults the giver, and the gifts dry up. As for the giver, a simple "you're welcome" to the response of "thank you" functions perfectly in the English-speaking world. No more. No less.

What for What?

We often get asked what value to assign to certain achievements. If only we all had one of those computers from Saturday morning cartoons where a lab-coated scientist would enter a string of computations, pull a lever, and out would pop a slip of paper containing the right answer. Unfortunately, important work on a potential gratitude computer never progressed, but we can give *you* a little programming.

Let's start with an example to plug into your computer: Juan in client relations takes Mark, a new employee, under his wing—explaining the ins and outs of the complex CRM system and answering all his questions with an infectious enthusiasm. Within just a few weeks Mark is operating independently and already a go-to member of the team. Juan deserves your gratitude, no doubt. But do you say thanks, write him a note, or send him scuba diving in the Maldives?

To understand the level of reward, we recommend deciding if the achievement is: 1) a small step toward living your values; 2) a one-time, larger achievement that reinforces your values and makes your team more successful; 3) an ongoing, above-and-beyond demonstration of your values in action; or 4) an achievement that has a significant impact on the bottom line.

Thus, the value of your expression of gratitude would fall into one of four categories: 1) praise-worthy, 2) reward-worthy, 3) platinum-level, and 4) diamond-level. Let us explain them a little more:

With praise-worthy gratitude, a manager encourages those little steps that lead a team to success. These are given to employees who meet performance expectations or do things within their job scope—get a report in on time, go out of their way to complete a delivery to a customer, show a positive attitude in a crisis, take a smart risk that doesn't quite work out, and so on. Gratitude at this level can be made publicly with verbal praise or by sending a handwritten or e-mailed note, or by giving something that has little value such as movie tickets, a favorite food item, or a coffee card.

Reward-worthy gratitude is for one-time stretch achievements that further your core values and make the team more successful. While praise is for meeting expectations, rewards are for something outside the typical job scope. This might be for an employee who serves on a cross-functional team, takes care of an important customer who is upset and is able to save the day, takes on an additional duty or works late to get out an important project or order, finds a way to improve a process or comes up with a creative solution to a problem, or maybe the team that puts together a great sales pitch for a prospective client. Most rewards at this level are less than one hundred dollars in value, and usually come in the form of something tangible that is meaningful to the person.

Platinum-level rewards are for those employees who display ongoing excellent work. Employees are eligible for this level of gratitude if they consistently demonstrate your values, for instance, by always being the one you turn to to take on challenging customer problems, or maybe they work extra shifts weeks in a row to cover for a coworker out on leave, or they toil long and hard to develop sophisticated changes to improve an important process that will have a big impact on team efficiency, or maybe they always demonstrate outstanding mentorship to new people on the team. If you just know at 5:05 p.m., after closing, that Susan doesn't hesitate to open the doors when a frantic customer shows up, she is most likely worthy of platinum-level gratitude and public recognition. If you want to put a dollar amount to this, the value would be less than five hundred dollars.

Diamond-level gratitude is reserved for behaviors that produce significant financial benefits for the organization. These rewards recognize an employee who has done something that makes a big impact to your bottom line: Perhaps developing a new system that saves the company money, being granted a patent, winning an industry award, breaking a performance record, landing a big new client, achieving a top sales goal, being part of a team that came together with the innovative pitch that won a big deal, working to save an important customer who had one foot out the door . . . you get the idea. Since these awards may be commensurate with the achievement, a cash component may be included, but there usually should be a tangible reminder of the achievement and a public recognition moment as well.

WE SPOKE WITH a technology employee who recalled an achievement he completed that we believed would classify as diamond-level. He had volunteered to put in double time to correct his organization's reporting software, which had been found to be inaccurate, and it had taken him a month of very late nights and weekends working in the office. "Our clients told us that if we didn't get it right, right away, they would cancel their contracts with us. It was a deal-breaker," he said. The employee explained that before he started the project, his boss made it clear that there would be a big reward at the end. When the project was completed, he waited . . . and waited. Finally, he went into his boss's office and asked if he should expect anything.

"She said, 'Oh yeah, that's right. Well, I would have to get it approved by the CEO,'" the employee said. The boss then asked the man if he wanted her to go ahead and ask for it. Yes, he said, that would be nice since it had been promised. "She told me she'd let me know when it was approved."

More weeks passed until his boss finally came by his cube and said a cash bonus had been approved. "But by then, instead of feeling excited, I kind of felt like, 'Well, it's about time,'" he said.

She said the bonus would likely be included in his next

paycheck or the one after that. The coup de grâce: A few weeks later he received a call from the company's payroll clerk, who asked him why he was getting an extra amount on his check. Embarrassed, he had to explain the project bonus. She hung up curtly, saying that it was highly irregular. *Okay.*

"Finally my wife called to let me know that the bonus had shown up on my paycheck," he said. "She was the one who said, 'You deserved it.'" There was no public commendation, no feeling of achievement and pride, and no reinforcement of his above-and-beyond actions that other employees could learn from.

This fellow turned out to be better at gratitude than his boss. Despite his disappointment, he bought a card and wrote a note to thank his manager for her efforts in getting him the bonus and presented it to her the next day with a verbal thank-you.

Gratitude Is Not a Generic Good

When it comes to expressions of gratitude, a generic thank-you isn't anywhere near as good as a custom offering. Tossing out a bunch of random *attaboys* can actually irritate people who work for you. Generic praise not only has little to no meaning, it tends to anger people over time because it's seen as disrespectful and careless. And yet we've probably all known a boss who sprayed the team with platitudes such as "Good job, everyone!" as he cruised through the cubicle maze on his way to more important uses of his time, possibly meeting with higher-ups to take credit for your work. You almost expect him to add, "Good job, everyone . . . *for whatever it is you do.*"

Leaders who spray their teams with the equivalent of gratitude air-freshener think they are being magnanimous, but they actually come across as either oblivious, with no idea of the specific tasks their people are accomplishing and how difficult the work is, or callous and unmoved by the emotional needs of their people. For example, saying, "Thanks for that report," is nice but a bit hollow, while saying, "Thanks for that report. Your work is always well-researched and accurate. You have an attention to detail that is hard to find," helps people understand the value they are bringing to their work. After all, which would you prefer to hear?

Dr. David Cherrington, a professor of organizational leadership at Brigham Young University, gave us a terrific example of how important this concept is not only at work but in our personal lives. In a workshop he was conducting at one company, Cherrington outlined this idea of specific praise and got some pushback from a man in the group. The fellow argued, as many managers have with us, that any kind of praise has a positive impact in a workplace, and he said he often threw out such positives as "good job" to his employees and they certainly seemed to appreciate his sentiments.

Cherrington asked if the man was a father. The fellow said yes, he had three children at home. The professor asked if he could conduct an experiment that night and report back to the group the next day. The man was to express appreciation to each of his three kids individually in the presence of his wife. He was to make this simple statement: "I just want you to know how much I appreciate everything you do," then leave the room, adding nothing more.

"After the father made the comment and left, his wife asked their youngest child why the father might have expressed appreciation," said Cherrington. "The ten-year-old replied, 'I guess he must be upset because I didn't get the dishes done like I was supposed to.'" Yikes, 180 degrees different than the reaction his father was expecting.

As to the fellow's thirteen-year-old, she replied to her mother, "I don't know why he said that; I guess he was just feeling sentimental." Not bad, but certainly not what the father was seeking.

By the time the dad met with his fifteen-year-old, he wondered if adding sincerity might pull this experiment out of the crapper. So, channeling his best William Shatner, he gave a moving performance, sighing to his oldest daughter, "Becky . . . I just want you to know how much I appreciate everything you do." Dad, appearing to struggle to contain his emotions, then left the room.

Mom asked Becky what she thought her father had meant by that statement. In a few brilliant words the daughter captured what a lot of employees are thinking: "Who knows, Mom? I don't think Dad has a clue what's going on around here."

Ah, the wisdom of youth.

For a great example of getting specificity right, consider this highly effective brief episode of gratitude we observed not long ago. A smart manager had gathered her group together and was thanking her seven team members, one at a time, for their work on a project. What we were particularly struck by was that she mentioned each person's particular contributions and based the remarks largely on their personalities. To a woman with a more self-assured nature, the leader said, "Cindy, I want to thank you for getting the momentum going with the analysis. We needed your insights and your direction, and this whole thing wouldn't have gotten off the ground without that pre-work," while to a more laid-back young man she said, "Jered, you kept the peace in the team when things got crazy stressful. Am I right, everyone? [Heads nodded.] We needed your steadying influence."

We found her specific words made this moment so much more memorable. We can still vividly recall the looks on the faces of her people as they realized she had noticed each of them and appreciated the work they had contributed. She demonstrated that she really knew them and valued distinctive features of their working styles that they had brought to the project.

No Daunting Task

We understand that the concept of tailoring gratitude might sound overwhelming to a busy leader. How's a manager supposed to know how to personalize rewards and words, especially if she's managing twenty people, or a team that includes those who aren't her direct reports? Good points. These are among the main reasons we developed the Motivators Assessment. When managers have their people take it, it leads to rich discussions in which gratitude (as well as other things such as career development) can be tailored to match the person's specific drivers.

We have seen other great approaches, too. Take the case of technology company Button in New York City. On their very first day, employees there are asked to fill out a survey that has them recall, in detail, a time they felt appreciated for their work. Based on the specifics gleaned, managers can better customize recognition celebrations for each—public or private, tangible award or experience, etc. So dang smart. And easy.

Another terrific idea we found speaking with Paul Hewitt, chief of the Park City (Utah) Fire District. Before coming on board from an out-of-state agency, he asked for pictures of all ninety of his employees-to-be, put them on flash cards, and memorized each face and name. He also asked each member of the team to write up a SWOT analysis of the department for him to review before he got there, including their ideas for improvements. "Just like a father should know his kids, a boss should know his employees on a professional and personal level," he said. This has led to useful discussions about where the department can improve service to residents as well as the work experience for the firefighters, and Hewitt's expressions of gratitude have been much more specific to each person in his crew.

One more fun example comes from Brad White, who will never forget receiving a personalized reward on his ten-year work anniversary as vice president of sales at AddVenture Products in San Diego. The company's owner, Alan Davis, presented his salesman with two baseballs autographed by White's favorite player, former Major League Baseball star Rickey Henderson. "I stood in front of the entire company accepting this gift, completely awestruck, honored, shocked, grateful, and thrilled," White said. "The value of having an employer who truly cares for you, who knows who you are as a person, and who goes the extra mile to show their appreciation, that value can't be measured."

Tailor to the Individual

- Not everyone in a leader's care appreciates the same rewards and often values very different things from their leader.
- Research shows all humans share a group of twenty-three motivators at work. The nuances in a person's specific nature show up in which of these are most important and the order of priority. Smart leaders use the knowledge of individual motivators to tailor expressions of gratitude to each team member.
- To understand the level of reward, decide if the achievement is: 1) a step toward living your values; 2) a one-time, larger step that reinforces your values; 3) an ongoing above-and-beyond demonstration of your values in action; or 4) an achievement that has a significant impact on the bottom line.
- "Thank you" is the only response necessary to gratitude. When we are ungrateful for gratitude, it diminishes the gift, insults the giver, and the gifts dry up.

Chapter 15

Reinforce Core Values

A common theme we heard from many of the leaders we interviewed: Expressions of gratitude should be connected to behaviors that are in line with the company or team core values. Appreciation, they said, is a powerful way to reinforce the importance of those vital principles.

Indeed, focused and specific gratitude can solve a big issue we see in many organizations: Leaders spend a lot of time carefully crafting a set of core values, communicating them to one and all, and yet the ideas haven't really come alive as a basic manner of operating, every day in every little way. They're just platitudes framed and hung around the hallways.

One problem: Leaders don't often exhibit the values themselves, at least not consistently. Another one: There's often little more than lip service given to the ideas. Leaders held a company meeting to unveil them and might even have handed out cards that employees are supposed to keep in their wallets and perhaps pull out when faced with a moral dilemma—"Hold on, Cliff, I need to check the values statement before I steal this photocopier."

A statement of values doesn't speak loudly enough.

One manager told us in all seriousness, "We printed wallet cards; everybody got one. Every one of our conference rooms has a framed poster with the values." He was flummoxed that, nonetheless, his people's behavior didn't conform to those stated values.

There is wisdom in the old adage "Actions speak louder than words." Not only must leaders act in accord with values themselves, they've got to demonstrate they truly appreciate employees enacting them as well.

Showing gratitude is one of the most effective and memorable ways to reinforce leadership's commitment to values and offers powerful opportunities to communicate why these grand ideals are so important—not to mention what can go wrong if they aren't demonstrated. Gratitude offers an opportunity to put the flesh of specificity on the bones of core values.

Now and then we've been asked to help recraft organizational mission, vision, and values statements to better define who the firm is, where they are going, and how they'll get there. To understand the culture better, we'll conduct employee focus groups first. And we can hear some skepticism about the values. "We're skeptical," they say (somewhat unimaginatively). Some of that seems to be an upshot of the vagueness of the values themselves. One company had advocated values that included teamwork and accountability. One employee complained, "No one has ever said *how* they want us to show these; like, they've never defined teamwork. Does that mean teamwork with the people in my department or with other groups around here, because we don't do that? And do they know sometimes teamwork really screws everything up? A lot of the times I slow down and try to get other people involved it can turn into this whole big thing. It stalls everything, and I just wish I'd done whatever I was doing by myself." Another employee added, "I wonder about accountability. We've got a guy on the team who I know is slacking off. Am I supposed to rat him out? Is that accountability?"

What's a Manager to Do?

What should managers do to provide clarity? Maybe hand out a PowerPoint detailing all sorts of specifics? Actually . . . that idea may not be so odd. When Netflix CEO Reed Hastings posted to the web a 125-page slide share called the Netflix Culture Deck, it became a phenomenon, viewed tens of millions of times. Hastings and his head of HR, Patty McCord, along with other members of the executive team, crafted the deck over years and walked people through it in intensive new hire meetings. What made the deck so effective is that it described the specific behaviors expected of all staff, expressing values as actions such as "Think strategically and articulate what you are, and *are not*, trying to do" and "Maintain calm poise in stressful situations." If you haven't read the deck, we recommend you google it and review it.

Of course, such elaborate and well-articulated communication about values is Holy Grail rare, which is one reason the Netflix deck has been so eagerly gobbled up by people around the world. We crave such specificity. If you're in the executive suite—or your senior leaders are receptive to such recommendations—you may want to help your organization craft such a document. We helped a large bank do just that recently, working with teams of employees around the world to come up with the expected behaviors for what they called their seven "enablers"—their core values that *enabled* them to live the company mission. Training sessions with all employees included brainstorming on how each person could live the expected values and behaviors in their jobs. As one IT employee told us after a session, "This is the first time I've really understood how my job can impact the bigger bank."

Even with such aids, in order for the values to be instilled as day-to-day operating norms, positive reinforcement of actual behaviors is essential by leaders. For this book, we had the privilege to interview Frances Hesselbein, who was called by management guru Peter Drucker "the best leader I've ever known." Hesselbein, the 103-year-old former CEO of the Girl Scouts of the USA, explained to us that values have to be linked to actions to make them habits. "We find leaders who are values-based, mission-focused, and demographic-driven are grateful," she said. "We find these leaders live with gratitude through their language and their actions. They are the leaders of the future. Without gratitude, we find leaders of the past."

One of the great payoffs for managers of this practice of connecting gratitude to values is the joy of continually observing just how many creative ways their people exhibit desired behaviors. We'll always remember how one laundry employee at a hotel chain was rewarded for living the firm's value of integrity. She had found a large bundle of cash stuffed in a guest's pillowcase that had come down to the laundry for cleaning. She rushed to her manager's office, burst in, and reported the finding. The manager happened to be in with an upset guest at the time. It seemed the man had lost a sum of money in his room. Long story short, the cash and guest were reunited, and the laundry employee was recognized for her integrity in front of the entire hotel staff.

Now, we are not sure what kind of "business" this guest was involved in if he carried around large wads of cash and stuffed them into pillowcases—so it was probably a wise idea to return the dough, if you catch our meaning. But still, what a terrific learning moment it was as the manager said in his expression of public gratitude: "Integrity is essential. If our guests can't trust the hotel, they won't stay here—it's that simple."

For Us as for You

Another employee pushback to corporate value statements is that tucked away inside is the presumption that leadership has to tell people the right way to live. We're not saying companies shouldn't have or communicate values; we actually think it's a vital practice. But it's important to clarify to employees that these values are here to guide everyone's behavior—leaders, employees, and the organization as whole. And we've seen consistently in our work that most employees want dearly to work for a company that has values and honors them. There is no better way to assure employees of that than to openly, consistently show appreciation for those who uphold these values.

One leader who shared this sentiment is Henry Timms. When he was president and CEO of the 92nd Street Y, a cultural and community center on the Upper East Side of Manhattan, he was deeply impressed by employees' commitment to their mission. He told us, "We aren't trying to flog a toothpaste the world doesn't need. We are about trying to make people's lives happier, more connected to each other, and help them find the gifts inside themselves. That means every day, every member of the staff comes through the doors trying to make people's lives better."

That desire to do work that is in service of others is ubiquitous in the workplace. Today's workforce is so enamored of aligning their values to the organization's that a whopping 95 percent of job candidates say they believe culture is more important than compensation, according to a Johns Hopkins University study. It's almost a given today that potential new hires will check you out extensively on the Internet, social media, and career sites. And what are they looking for? First, who do you profess to be (that's your brand), and second, do people who work for you think you live up to what you pro-fess (that's your culture)?

When gratitude is consistently and meaningfully given to those who live the values, team members become your greatest advocates. A host of positive employee comments about an organization and culture on social media and career websites is priceless—helping recruiting efforts and building a brand as a top choice for candidates. Another plus: Poten-tial hires have a clear understanding of what to expect before joining, which means leaders (and they) can better evalu-ate fit during the interview process, saving everyone a lot of time and effort. Netflix has found that its Culture Deck has been a powerful magnet to attract high-quality employees, a benefit they hadn't expected. Applicant after applicant be-gan saying they'd sent in their résumés because they liked what the deck suggested the company aspired to be.

What follows are our best tips for tying gratitude to team or organizational values. We recommend starting before a new employee does.

Kicking It Off Pre-Hire

The most vital step in bringing core values alive in a culture is finding ways to inculcate them into employees' day-to-day work. When it's done right, that starts before a person even joins the company, in the hiring process, by sharing stories about how these concepts have been applied by other workers.

It then continues on day one with a robust way of helping new employees understand the relevance of the values and what they should expect when they get to work—and what they shouldn't. Quicken Loans founder Dan Gilbert and CEO Bill Emerson, for instance, personally spend a full day in every new employee orientation going over their company's culture and nineteen values. The company also annually publishes a values-in-action book.

Gail Miller, owner of the Larry H. Miller Group of Companies, told us, "We try to get people engaged from day one in our values and understand what they mean and where they came from. That creates loyalty, gratitude for the job, and gratitude that we are associating with people of like-mindedness." The values Miller's company promotes are integrity, hard work, service, and stewardship. While the concepts they're presented with are simple, new employees are given specific examples in training that explain how others have demonstrated these ideals in their work, and how each of them can incorporate the values into their daily tasks.

Your organization may not have such a concerted initiation process. Some organizations spend new employee orientation focused almost exclusively on the company history, products and services, or safety rules, with little explicitly said about values. If so, managers can make up for this by having a thoughtful one-on-one review with those joining their teams—going into more detail about how they hope employees will emulate the values.

Stories are the best way to convey that these ideas truly

matter and to clarify how they can be lived. We heard one impressive instance at an oil and gas company new employee orientation, where the facilitator told the story of one of their oil field technicians (whom they call pumpers) arriving to check one of the company's nodding-donkey wells in the Colorado high desert. The pumper found the well surrounded by three feet of water—from the spring runoff—and realized it would be impossible for him to drive out there and take his readings or fix anything that might be broken.

Said the facilitator, "Our pumper went back down the road, borrowed a rowboat from a rancher, and rowed out to check the well. Everything was okay, and he was able to continue on his shift. When I heard this story, I thought it was such a terrific example of living our core values." She then asked the participants which of the company's values they thought might have been at play in this situation. A robust discussion quickly ensued in which the new employees mentioned "resourcefulness" and "safety" most frequently.

Another point we make as we help inculcate values within an organization is for leadership to prioritize them to help resolve value conflicts that may come up for their people. Say a core value is "speed," and another "ethical behavior." Well, in the pursuit of rapidly responding to a customer request or getting a new product to market, is it possible that an employee might cut a corner? Absolutely. Or how about values of "accountability" and "excellence"? In their eagerness to hit a deadline to be *accountable*, could employees sacrifice quality and *excellence*? Again, no doubt. That's why we always recommend values be rank-ordered, so that, for instance, employees would understand that ethical behavior would trump speed in that scenario, and excellence would overrule accountability in the latter. We also recommend leaders help their people understand the most common values-driven conflicts and provide ways to deal with them.

Managers can also make it clear that if anyone is confronting a values conflict, they should seek them out for counsel. And when they do, the employees should be shown fulsome gratitude for doing so.

One last point here we must acknowledge is that there are times when living company values might violate an employee's personal values, which does happen more often than we may think. A friend of ours works for an insurer that lists "profitable growth" among its core values. Nothing wrong with growing, of course. They are a public company, and shareholders demand growth on their investments. But with this value, it's assumed that the company expects to increase bottom-line profits each year, and that means it's going to live the letter of the law when it comes to what claims it approves. No wiggle room. Our friend has said how hard it can be on her personally when she has to decline a claim. One form of gratitude is for leaders to display empathy about how hard such things are for their people. The key is to help employees understand and respect the values, even if they may not completely agree with them, and empathetically understand why values-based decisions may be hard on them.

Ask the Team to Tie Appreciation to Values

At a large investment management firm where we were about to conduct a leadership workshop, we learned the organization had a great way of reinforcing behaviors that were aligned with its values. As we were touring the cubicle plains, we were struck by all the thank-you cards and printed-out electronic notes of thanks papering employee workspaces. Some forty thousand were sent in the first year after the company's Spotlight Program was introduced, the vice president of client communication told us.

The firm's leadership had set up the program after asking employees through an electronic survey what they could do to improve the culture. The two most frequent answers from the typically staid credit analysts, compliance officers, and portfolio managers were "have more fun" and "recognize our work." Who'd have thunk it? The leaders smartly spotted an opportunity to add some reinforcement of their stated values into the mix. When introducing the program, the leadership asked that colleagues explain in printed cards or electronic spotlight notes to their fellow workers how the other associates have demonstrated service, teamwork, leadership, or innovation.

The VP explained that the program was indeed making this buttoned-down workplace a lot more fun and rewarding. It also had done a great job of reinforcing the kinds of behaviors they most wanted to see, which made it popular with the executive team, too. "It's working," she said. "We have seen our client satisfaction scores go up, and associates are just happier and feel more appreciated."

The takeaway for any leader in this process is to help employees understand how to tie their peer-to-peer gratitude to the team or organizational values, and for the leader to model the behavior herself.

Rituals Provide Opportunities to Live the Values

WD-40 Company CEO Garry Ridge told us about a great way he's helped his team connect one of its core values—"Creating positive lasting memories in all our relationships"—with expressions of gratitude. Each year Ridge brings together his extended leadership team for a retreat to build memories. A culminating event is a gathering under the stars where people sit around a campfire and write on a piece of paper something they are grateful for that happened during the previous year or, in some cases, something they want to let go of: a grudge, a habit, a mistake, etc. They then throw the piece of paper into the fire.

Often participants share their story of gratitude (though there is no pressure to do so). Ridge said one of the leaders at a recent fireside explained how vulnerable she'd been when her mother died and how grateful she was to her coworkers. "I needed the help of my tribe, and you didn't let me down," she said as she tossed her piece of paper into the fire. "I'm so grateful to all of you. Today I'm letting go of my grief and committing to be there for others as you were there for me this last year."

Ridge says moments of gratitude like this help move people from feeling their work is a mindless ritual to "a sacred duty, shared with other humans, and has created special memories that have bonded people to each other."

Ken Chenault told us a ritual he kept up while CEO of American Express was brown-bag lunches with employees around the world. He saw these as a chance to reinforce the company's Blue Box core values, answer questions, and explain to his people the rationale behind decisions that were being made at the corporate level. "If people see a caring criteria is put in place, they get a sense of how your decisions and actions are guided by core values," he said.

At the end of the meetings, Chenault would then ask a favor of the attendees: "Tell a few other people in the company what you thought of our meeting. Anything you want. You can say, 'Ken is a jerk, I didn't agree with him,' but it's important that people know I'm a human being, that you interacted with me, and so anything you say I would be thankful for. Those stories spread in the company, so that when I would go to a Town Hall, or hold a satellite Town Hall, people had a sense of who I was that was supplemented by these personal stories."

At another company, a value was "seeing the best in one another." As such, the day before we arrived at their annual meeting to speak, the team had spent the day working around the city in various service opportunities. We heard from several people that a tough-as-nails division VP had scooped out mashed potatoes at the homeless shelter, and her team members were still buzzing about how cool it was to see the warmer side of her. In turn, this executive had been so moved that she had actually thanked her team for doing a great job and linked it to them seeing the best in those they had served that day.

Connect to Values in Formal Celebrations

Gail Miller told us about a great way her company ties gratitude to what matters most. Every year it hosts a system-wide presentation on the mission, vision, and values—where leaders publicly highlight the stories of employees who have brought these concepts to life. The employees or teams are then publicly commended and rewarded for their actions.

"We had a young woman join our prime finance company, a single mom, who felt out of place at first," said Miller. "The team rallied around her, made her feel welcome, helped her learn her job. Today she's a loyal and happy employee because her team members served her, and we recognized them for their efforts. We've also thanked employees who've displayed hard work by going the extra mile to fix customers' cars, and we recognized the guy who runs our theaters, who is always going the second mile."

Miller's example is one every manager can emulate. Huddles, staff meetings, performance reviews, and every other chance to gather with employees is an opportunity to provide gratitude to those who live the values. Leadership gurus Jim Kouzes and Barry Posner articulate this beautifully when they suggest tying expressions of gratitude to values is one of the best ways of "heightening awareness of an organization's expectations and humanizing the values such that we motivate at a deep and enduring level."

Reinforce Core Values

+ Even though core values may have been communicated to employees, the ideas often don't come alive in day-to-day behaviors. Expressions of gratitude, when connected to actions that are in line with the company or team core values, offer powerful opportunities to communicate why these grand ideals are so important.

+ Today's workforce is so enamored of aligning their values to the organization's that 95 percent of job candidates say they believe culture is more important than compensation. Employees want to know 1) who do you profess to be (your brand) and 2) do you live up to what you profess (your culture).

+ Leaders should rank-order values to help resolve conflicts that may come up for their people. They can also help their people understand common values-driven conflicts and provide ways to deal with them.

+ Living a company value might violate a personal value for an employee. One form of gratitude is when leaders display empathy about how hard such things are for their people and help them understand and respect the values, even if they may not completely agree with them.

Chapter 16

Make It Peer-to-Peer

Manager-to-employee and peer-to-peer gratitude fulfill separate human needs. When employees are grateful to each other, they affirm positive, vital concepts typically valued in their colleagues such as trustworthiness, dependability, and talent. Peer-to-peer gratitude is particularly powerful because it comes from the people who are most respected—their fellow team members. And this can have an invigorating effect on organizations overall.

Part of the success of JetBlue Airlines comes from their focus on social, peer-to-peer recognition, says Shawn Achor, author of *The Happiness Advantage*. At JetBlue, which has been named by J.D. Power as the highest in customer satisfaction among low-cost carriers for eleven years running, coworkers can nominate other crew members for everyday contributions as well as above-and-beyond work or effort through a program called Lift. Successes are shared throughout the company on an internal newsfeed. You want numbers? JetBlue data shows that for every 10 percent increase in people reporting being recognized, it sees a 3 percent increase in employee retention and a 2 percent increase in engagement.

In addition to being good for business and people, gratitude between team members also assures people that their coworkers have their backs. Our surveys show most engaged employees agree with the statement "My teammates support each other." This reinforces the vital concept of psychological safety. In the best teams, employees feel free to speak up, share ideas, and know that they can ask others for help and not get laughed at for being a wuss. As part of creating such safety on a team, Alan Mulally told us, "There is never a joke at anybody's expense. Never, ever. People may go along to get along, but it's never funny and it's poison in a working-together environment. If people feel they could be a victim, they are going to be really careful about what they share about their real situation."

It's about Everyone

There are reasons peer-to-peer gratitude is becoming popular. A Simply Talent poll of 1,500 employees across Europe found that peers have the biggest influence on employee engagement levels—twice as important as line managers—and a separate study found companies with peer-to-peer recognition systems are 35 percent more likely to report lower employee turnover.

Henry Timms, president and CEO of Lincoln Center, has an interesting way of discussing how leaders might think about this idea of team gratitude. "I think a culture of gratitude is a story that people appreciate each other," he said. "In one version of this story, Leader A is a great leader: He always expresses gratitude; he always says thank you to the intern. That's fine. But what we would seek for is Story B, a culture where gratitude is about everybody. It's not a leader-follower dynamic but a culture for the whole institution. In a perfect institution, there would be a context of gratitude that would exist at every level."

That may sound like a rosy ideal, but we've seen the power of what Timms describes in action. Members of the best teams don't wait for their leaders to say thanks; they take the initiative. In the majority of cases, it's in the form of simple praise and is informal, which means it costs little or nothing.

If a leader actively encourages peer-to-peer appreciation, it can become a practice team members commit to and are thoughtful about. Adrian had the pleasure of witnessing an example of The Culture Works team formally showing each other gratitude, even though he wasn't supposed to be there. He had been out of town working with a client. The work had ended ahead of schedule, and he had caught an early flight home. He swung by the office unexpectedly and found the team members standing in a group, and the head of training, Chris Kendrick, was in the middle of recognizing logistics manager Bri Bateman for the ownership she had displayed. Just a few days before, Chris had arrived in a faraway city for a client presentation and realized his training materials had not arrived. Bri saved his bacon. She found an overnight delivery service office near the airport that could take late shipments and dashed out there. By the next morning, Chris had his materials and was able to wow as always.

What struck us about this scene was, as the owners of the company, we weren't invited, didn't approve anything, and weren't needed. And that was just fine. Gratitude was happening without us, and it was aligned to something that really mattered to the team—ownership of an issue.

We've found that getting the practice of peer-to-peer gratitude to take hold in a team does take a little effort on the part of leaders. It's our job to help employees understand how it should work. Some managers have told us that they've tried this, but their people ended up thanking each other for silly things such as, and we quote, "sharing your lunch" or being "super fun." It's great if team members are friendly, of course, but those examples of gratitude are clearly not what we are talking about.

Good modeling is one way to assure your people understand what you're looking for, and we find that leaders see a natural ripple effect with their teams. We advise taking a more formal approach and talking with your team about why it's important they tie peer-to-peer gratitude to core values and how to do it right.

Socializing Recognition

We recommend a leader make use of one of the online systems or apps that have been developed to facilitate team-based gratitude. They're called social recognition systems. A research team from the University of Washington, MIT, and Microsoft Corporation found, "Appreciation systems—a genre of messaging and microblogging systems that mediate digital expressions of appreciation in the workplace—have become widely adopted in recent years. Thirty-five percent of companies used some form of online peer recognition system in 2015, an approach that was overtaking top-down recognition efforts."

These systems can help build bonds outside of immediate teams, break down silos, and help workers in different locations feel more connected to one another. Social recognition also helps remote workers, who often feel left out, feel more included. Of course, managers shouldn't just leave this to their teams but should participate in the system as well. When managers recuse themselves from the process (or regularly use words like *recuse*), they become less a part of the team—embodying the "them" in the us-versus-them scenario.

The researchers found the thanks messages in social recognition systems were most often sent to coworkers outside of one's own team. Employees said they wanted the other team member's manager to see the thanks they were sending, "and most managers do report seeing the messages and mentioning them to team members," the report said. Unfortunately, while users had high expectations for the effect of their messages on the colleague's managers, the researchers found a large group of leaders ignored appreciation reports and did not use them to inform decisions or performance reviews. Shame. Wasted opp.

We've seen a wide range of approaches to making use of social recognition. We've mentioned JetBlue's program, for instance, which can record and track data and help identify top performers, known as "influencers," who wow clients every day. The company has been able to spend more time with these special employees and learn from them how they are able to maintain enthusiasm to serve customers in an often challenging industry.

At Bonusly, which has offices in Colorado and New York as well as remote employees around the world, each employee is given a budget and asked to find ways to celebrate other team members through the year. When a colleague does express gratitude to another for doing something valuable, the entire team is notified on a dashboard and gets a chance to join in on the celebration. To make sure everyone knows of the great work that's going on—despite the distance that separates them—they maintain an online dashboard that displays all the gratitude that happens during the day. They are trying to encourage more expressions of thanks by putting power into the hands of everyone, making gratitude more visible, frequently given, and specific to what matters most. (And no, if you're wondering, employees don't get to keep any money they don't use.)

Of course, it's not necessary to use a commercially designed program. At The Culture Works, we use a Slack channel for gratitude. Typically it is used as a work-sharing, collaboration tool, but we've found it's a terrific resource for thanks. The channel buzzes all day with messages as our teammates cheer each other's client successes. Positive reviews of trainings and other accolades are shared for all, and there is a pile-on effect as people chime in with their congratulations in real time. This has been a terrific way to keep our remote and gig employees connected to the team as well. For instance, when our web developer Bryce recently completed an upgrade that allowed for the automated fulfillment of orders (instead of the manual way we'd been doing things), the Slack channel went wild with members of the team thanking him and telling him specifically how that would impact their jobs and free them up to do other work.

Another great use of freely available online technology is posting complimentary videos of one of your fellow star employees on YouTube or the company intranet. To celebrate teammate Michael Andersen-Leavey's winning of the Pinnacle Award—one of the highest employee honors at American Express—his colleagues created a carpool karaoke parody video of "Nothing's Gonna Stop Us Now" and posted it on their intranet. His fellow HR professionals from around the world drove together while singing modified lyrics to the Starship song to celebrate Andersen-Leavey's competency at implementing new processes and policies and helping internal groups get through audits.

Dave Zielinski, writing for SHRM, warns that while

social recognition can be a boon for employee engagement, there are some practices to avoid. These include use of restrictive reward tactics like gamification concepts in which employees are given points for recognizing the work of others—a practice that can result in people rushing to send out halfhearted "Nice work" messages by program deadlines. He also says executives and managers at all levels must support the program and use it themselves.

Laura Sejen, managing director at Willis Towers Watson, adds that it's important social recognition be nonbureaucratic, that the process to nominate coworkers is easy, and that the program is well-publicized throughout the organization. "Sometimes employees aren't even aware these programs exist, so it's important to communicate about them and give them a higher profile," she said.

No Technology Required

If you're not enamored of online tools, or your superiors aren't going to approve the idea, no worries. Good old-fashioned tangible tools can do the trick. Because so much communication is online nowadays, handwritten notes can be one of the most meaningful forms of gratitude. Taking the time and making the effort to "go analog" and write with a pen boosts the gratitude factor by a ton. We encourage leaders to provide various kinds of simple tools for this, such as giving employees a stack of thank-you notes. We've done this, and our team's bulletin boards are packed with notes that have meant a lot to them.

Another idea: At software company Typeform, anyone in the office can start a round of applause for another staff member when they've done something noteworthy, and everyone joins in. They call it "spontaneous applause," and it is part of their team culture. And no, it doesn't get out of hand (sorry).

At online retailer Zappos, we once talked about the concept of getting peers involved in gratitude with senior director of customer service Rob Siefker. He told us his team did SNaPS recognition, which stood for Super Nifty and Positive Stuff. He said employees wrote down things that others do during the day that are "really cool" and put those notes into a SNaPS box. "These are read out loud during our Zuddles [a Zappos huddle]. Then the person is publicly recognized on the spot. It's peer-to-peer. Then we all snap our fingers," he said, happily demonstrating to us.

We know many leaders might not want their workplaces to take on the appearance of a graduation-night kegger. Maybe applause and SNaPS are over the top for some. No problem. There are so many other ways to facilitate meaningful expressions of gratitude peer-to-peer.

Another great approach we've seen is to provide some fun little tchotchke, toy, or doodad that can become a gratitude trophy. One of the most memorable examples we've heard of was shared by the manager of a technology group at a large logistics company. This leader told us about finding his boyhood G.I. Joe action figure when he visited his parents' house. He thought it would be a hoot if he brought the doll into work and set it on his desk. After all, Joe had saved the world a million times over in his backyard—what could the bearded soldier with the kung fu grip accomplish in a multinational corporation's IT department?

So there Joe sat, day after day, until one day he was just gone.

"I guessed that someone on the team maybe thought he was a little odd, so they got rid of him," the leader told us. But he was wrong. It seemed his team members liked Joe a lot, and they had borrowed him to use as a traveling award. The rules, the team had decided, were simple: Whoever received the action figure—renamed the "You Da' Man" award—had to have done something that helped support another team member. No hogging Joe was another rule: The employee who got him would keep the award for a few days and then had to pass it on to a coworker who demonstrated another value that moved the team closer to their goals.

A few of the proud employees even brought the doll to team meetings when they had him, and no visitor could resist passing Joe on a worker's desk without a comment. Each person in turn took pride in displaying the symbol of peer recognition (not a single one hid the little soldier under their desk). And, in turn, team members learned a lot about where they were going and what it took to get there.

While a touring action figure might not be your team's cup of tea, you can surely find some fun object that would be meaningful to them—we've seen everything from old bowling trophies to rubber chickens. Try to find something that relates to the work you do.

THE WHOLE IDEA of making it peer-to-peer is to have a little more fun with your team. We give you permission to lighten up. In fact, that's just about a necessity in today's workplace, what with all the stress and pressure. If you've felt about ready to surrender to the upturned schnozzes of the grumps of this world, please keep fighting.

After we speak at conferences and try to convince leaders to practice the soft stuff and inject a little humanity into their work, we are so touched that believers will often swim upstream through exiting conference attendees to shake our hands as if we're the handle on the last water pump in the Sahara. "Thank goodness you came," they'll say. "These guys really needed to hear this message; we're so bad at this stuff."

Here's what these converted have discovered: With sky-high competition for great talent today, having a little more fun at work can provide a serious competitive advantage, helping attract and retain the people you need and providing a spark to jump-start creativity.

In short, people tend to stay, stay committed, and give more energy in a team where a little fun is injected into their work.

Make It Peer-to-Peer

- Manager-to-employee and peer-to-peer gratitude fulfill separate human needs.
- When employees are grateful to each other, they affirm positive concepts typically valued in their colleagues, such as trustworthiness, dependability, and talent.
- Surveys show most engaged employees agree with the statement "My teammates support each other." This reinforces the concept of psychological safety. In the best teams, employees feel free to speak up, share ideas, and know they can ask others for help.
- Online systems or apps can facilitate peer-to-peer gratitude. These social recognition, peer recognition systems are overtaking top-down recognition efforts.
- Peer recognition can help build bonds outside of immediate teams, break down silos, and help workers in different locations feel more connected to one another.
- Practices to avoid include the use of gamification concepts in which employees are given points for recognizing the work of others. Executives and managers at all levels must also support the program and use it themselves. The process to nominate coworkers should be easy and nonbureaucratic.

Part III

A Grateful Life

Chapter 17

Take It Home

While one of our trainers was working with a group of managers in South Carolina, during lunch one day an attendee, whom we'll call Mike, said he wanted to tell our trainer a story. He'd worked a few years for his current boss, Phil, and liked the guy. Phil was smart, personable, and always found the time to help Mike out. Phil even regularly expressed gratitude for his employees' contributions.

Mike then said he had a brother who lived not far away from him in a nice gated community. The brother had mentioned he shared a fence line with a neighbor whom he called Mr. Grumpy Pants (actually, he used a more colorful moniker, but we don't want an R rating stamped on our book). Now, it was clear that this guy was one of those neighbors no one wants. If you accidently threw your Frisbee into his yard, you gave it up for lost. If on a snowy day a branch of a neighbor's tree bent over his fence, Mr. G. P. would cut it off.

Mike's brother had told him he felt bad for the guy's wife and daughter.

Our trainer nodded and asked Mike politely where he was going with this tale. Mike's face grew serious, and he said, "So a few weekends ago my brother invites me to a party at their clubhouse, and he points the grumpy neighbor out to me. I'm not messing with you. It was MY BOSS, PHIL!"

"It has really made me second-guess him," Mike continued. "I mean, is that weird or what? He's a completely different person out of here."

Unfortunately, leaders like Phil are not that rare. They give their best selves at work, but sometimes have little left over for the people who should mean the most in their lives. Phil was compartmentalizing: tough guy at home, chill at work. And, of course, we find the opposite just as common: grateful, gracious, respectful with friends and loved ones, while a complete tool on the job.

If we practice gratitude with all the people in our lives, we'll find that they respond just as well as our employees. When we give our family, friends, and all those we encounter a lift, we also give ourselves more moments of joy. One of the great ironies of personal relationships is that we so often take those who mean the most to us for granted. With such busy schedules and so much pressure at work, we're often out of gas by the time we make it home. We fall into ritual conversations or head right to the TV for some mindless relaxation.

"How was your day?"

"Fine."

"What do you feel like for dinner?"

"Whatever."

Before we know it, we forget to ask our daughter about her school project she'd been so worried about or the big meeting our spouse had been anxious about. A special meal labored over gets no consummate praise, and all that time trimming the lawn or folding laundry gets as little appreciation as does so much work at the office.

Practicing gratitude is such a simple way to reinvigorate our personal and social lives.

Dr. Annie McKee of the University of Pennsylvania wrote about a major turnaround in the life of one of her clients. Her coaching client, Miguel, was failing in his senior leadership role. McKee said, "When I asked him, 'Do you care about people?' He responded genuinely, 'I really don't. I care about results.'"

With that mountain to climb, she created a skills-building plan for the man to try to better lead his team members, but over several months he made only marginal progress. Then something happened. One Saturday, Miguel cancelled on his kids again and went in to the office to deal with a fire. While he was gone, all hell broke loose at home. The kids were sick of playing second fiddle. That night Miguel's wife sat him down and explained what he was doing to his children . . . and to her.

Knowing things were dire, he realized he had to change, and he was finally ready to start listening. He started observing what was really going on with his loved ones—seeing them, for the first time in years—and then was able to express his sincere gratitude for their important roles in his life. Miguel began to fix things with his family, and soon it hit him like a garden shovel to the base of his skull: He needed to do the same at work. He started to see better what was going on in his employees' worlds and then was able to help his team members feel more valued for their contributions. His team became more energized, and he was much more attentive and thoughtful at home, and much happier.

One of the most common sources of life dissatisfaction these days is the lack of quality time spent with those we love. As if e-mail and umpteen meetings weren't bad enough at work, at home now we've got devices stealing our attention. Kids are glued to YouTube or constantly Snapchatting with their friends. We adults communicate less voice-to-voice with others than ever before, instead sending emoji-laden texts that say we care.

While we don't pretend to have a magical means of bringing back the "good old days" where everyone sat around the living room having attentive, high-quality conversations (*Amos 'n' Andy* on the radio ended that forever), what we can say is that we've learned a number of terrific practices that very busy business leaders have implemented to ensure they're expressing gratitude to their loved ones regularly.

Take Time Once a Day to Reflect

When we coach people, we encourage them to maintain daily gratitude journals—writing down anything and everything they are thankful for at the end of each day. Even if you can't find time to do it daily, do it when needed, says New York City marketing company owner Dave Kerpen. "When I am in a bad mood, I walk away from the situation, open up the Notes on my phone, set the timer for two minutes, and start typing the things and people I'm grateful for," he said. "Two minutes later I come back to my team, or my family, or my wife, and I'm in a better mood—every single time."

Ameet Mallik, executive vice president and head of US Novartis Oncology, keeps a family gratitude journal that he opens up every few weeks and makes notes of what his family members are thankful for. "It's like unpeeling an onion because the big stuff comes out first: the vacation we took or the grandparent who visited. Eventually you start getting to the small stuff. That's when you realize what they really appreciate. Like my son will say at recess today his friend threw a pass and he got a touchdown, or my other son will say I got a cupcake from my piano teacher for doing a good job and it was amazing. That's where the best stuff is. These little moments of joy that you find in each day."

You can do this any way you like. Write notes on your mobile phone. Buy a special leather-bound notebook and keep it by your bed to make entries in every night. A wonderful practice our friend and agent, Jim Levine, shared with us is that he begins each day by dipping into what he calls his treasure chest in his home office. The box contains pictures of his grandchildren and children. He chooses one at random and writes in his journal what he remembers of that time together. Then later, before he goes to sleep at night, he jots down three things he's been the most grateful for that day. "I've got a limited time here; this is my trip to planet earth. I try every day to be grateful for what is special, meaningful, and joyous."

Research has shown that the power of keeping a gratitude journal is extraordinary. Robert Emmons, a professor at the University of California, Davis, points to the results of several studies of more than two thousand people to show the value. "The benefits from counting blessings are tangible, emotionally and physically," he said. "People are 25 percent happier and more energetic if they keep gratitude journals, have 20 percent less envy and resentment, sleep 10 percent longer each night and wake up 15 percent more refreshed, exercise 33 percent more, and show a 10 percent drop in blood pressure compared to persons who are not keeping these journals."

Personal stories always speak persuasively to us, so we'd like to share one told to us by author Rebekah Lyons. Nine years ago, she and her family moved to Manhattan. "We had three kids, two toy poodles, and a minivan . . . and minivans aren't cool anywhere, *especially* New York," she joked with us. Lyons's youngest child had just started kindergarten, and thus "I was ready to reawaken my passions and figure out how life would play out in New York City." Four months later she had her first panic attack. What began that day continued in planes, trains, elevators, subways, and crowds for the next year and a half.

Lyons said a gratitude journal helped her make it through. "I'm a person of faith, and I read the verse 'Be anxious for nothing, but in everything with prayer and petition, with thanksgiving, let your requests be known to God.' I thought: The key is not just to pray for relief of this anxiety, but to do it with a heart of gratitude. And so, the practical person I am, I started a gratitude journal immediately. I met my fear with gratitude."

Lyons would send off her kids to school, force herself out of her apartment to walk to the corner bakery or to yoga at the gym, and then would come back to her journal. "I would write out twenty things I was grateful for. The smallest things: my kids' smiles, the way they said goodbye, the way the dogs want to always hang out at my feet.

"My gratitude was birthed from that season of anxiety. I realized that if I want peace every day, then I need to invite it in."

A Baker's Dozen More Ways to Develop a Grateful Life

While journaling is fundamental, there are other great ways we've seen people develop depths of gratitude in their personal lives. As with our other suggestions in this book, it's up to you to decide which will work and which might not be for you, but we ask your indulgence to take a moment to consider each.

1. Make a commitment to give undivided attention to your loved ones.

One of the most powerful ways to express our gratitude with family members and close friends is to show we are serious about spending time with them. A number of busy leaders told us they have made such a commitment. One is former American Express CEO Ken Chenault, who said, "When you're a leader, time is precious. When I'm with my family, I really strive to devote 100 percent of my attention to the family. Since I've been very declarative about that, when I don't do it, they call me on it."

2. Have three things for dinner.

A few years ago, Dave Kerpen was frustrated by the typical dinner conversation with his kids. You know the drill: Parent: "How was your day?" Kids: "Fine." Parent: "What did you do?" Kids: "Nothing." So Kerpen instituted a practice where they go around the dinner table and each person says three things: their favorite moment of the day, one person they're grateful for who's not at the table, and one person that they're grateful for who's at the table who hasn't been thanked yet. Kerpen says his kids "crazy hated the idea at first, but now it's a practice we do every day and they're proud of it. I get a little teary-eyed. My kids went from cynical and dreading it to embracing it to the point where they share it with friends when they're over for dinner."

3. Be excited to see them.

To create a positive and consistent balance between work and life it's important to extend to your loved ones the same courtesies you extend to your officemates. So try greeting your family members with a smile-laced "Good morning." We let people know by our body language that we are grateful to see them. Now, we admit they may not care—especially the teens who'll think you're a nut job—but it really will do wonders for morale in the home.

4. Give immediate positive feedback to family members.

As we take some of the skills we learn at work to our homes, it's a good idea to teach yourself to give immediate positive feedback to loved ones—learning to say specific thanks right away. Also, work to be a more active listener with your family and more gracious when challenged, which includes acknowledging imperfections and even thanking loved ones for their gentle rebukes. Part of this skill is being present, closing laptops, and turning off your phones when with family and sacrificing some of your "you" time for them. This may mean learning to play video games with the kids and going to their games and school events. Heaven forbid you should show up a little late for work because you spent an hour at the elementary school watching your little pilgrims in a Thanksgiving skit. Take a walk around the neighborhood with your significant other and ask about their next big project. The better you get at noticing the great things your family members are doing the easier and more natural it will be at work.

5. Give them a break.

Kids are going to mess up. They're going to make you sick with worry. They won't make their beds. They won't eat vegetables. They'll torment their siblings. They won't clean up after the hamster after swearing they would. They'll refuse to shower. They'll shower too much. They'll take your money AND LIE ABOUT IT! What good is raging like a college basketball coach? Kids do this stuff. You did. We encourage those we coach to dig way down deep and be grateful for the lessons their family members are teaching them. And, of course, to let them know how much those loved ones mean to them.

6. Be more grateful to your partner.

Would your significant other be surprised to hear you in a conversation with your employees? Would he or she be hurt to see the attention you pay, the interest you convey, or the gratitude you give to Roger or Tina in accounting, but hardly ever at home? By a similar token, would your employees think aliens had replaced you with a clone if they visited you at your house and witnessed you praising your kids for their Rorschach-like finger paintings?

7. Practice random gratitude.

At least once a week we're out speaking to management groups somewhere on this globe, and we know that travelers do not smile. It's some kind of understood arrangement: no smiling on the plane, shuttle bus, or moving walkway. And no liquids, except in a plastic sandwich bag, which cannot contain an actual sandwich. So, we dare you to travel with a smile on your face. Not a Jack Nicholson "Here's Johnny!" smile from *The Shining*. Just a grin will do. Once you've tried that, bring the smile to your next visit to a shopping mall, grocery store, sporting event, or community barbecue. And, if we may add this: Try extra hard to remember to use people's names when greeting them.

8. Be grateful for obstacles.
When driving, remember that literally no one on the road has anything personal against us. All they care about is themselves. So be the grateful one. Go out of your way to thank people who let you into their lane. Smile and wave (all five fingers). Even be grateful for delays that give you more time with that vampire book on tape or the chance to sing along with a few more Mötley Crüe songs on satellite radio. Then, when you get where you are going, be kind to those who serve you in restaurants, stores, banks, and the like. Cut them some slack and thank them for even the smallest of kindnesses, even if it is their job. Don't allow minor flares of incompetence or undercooked entrées to put a damper on your day. You'll stand a better chance of avoiding "mystery ingredients" in your soufflé if you ease up and approach everything with an eye toward gratitude.

9. Teach your kids to give.

Billionaire Gail Miller has gotten her very large family involved in giving efforts "to build character and understand how grateful we are for what we have by sharing it with others." As such, she asks each of her grandchildren (a group she calls Miller 3.0) to find a need that resonates with them starting at age twelve. "They have to investigate it, see what the registered nonprofit would use the money for, and then come back and do a report to the family board. They're either granted or denied their request." If approved, the grandchild delivers the funding. "Their responsibility with this exercise is to bless those who don't have what they have," she added. While most of us might not have the assets of the Larry H. and Gail Miller Family Foundation, we still thought it was a terrific idea to get children involved in any philanthropic giving we are able to do, which will create more grateful hearts in the process.

10. Serve together.

Mark Cole, president of the John Maxwell Companies, looks for ways he and his family can donate an entire day of service together. "You know why?" he asked us. "Because it hurts. I'd rather be on vacation, or home resting, or out selling something. So, when I give service, I feel the pain. I wake up in the morning and say, 'Why did I agree to do this?' But the feeling is 180 degrees different by the end of those service days. I feel like I've done something generous by doing something for others they cannot do for themselves," he said.

11. Smell the roses.

Rebekah Lyons has learned to be grateful that her kids slow her down. She said, "I wake my kids up in the morning and they are all smiles and just so happy eating their peanut butter toast and fried eggs, and I'm looking at the clock like, 'We gotta go!' But they're savoring every moment. What do I need to learn from this? I need to give myself more time. I want to meet the day with the same kind of joy they have. I don't want to rush through life and realize I didn't stop and smell the roses." Designer and author Ayse Birsel told us of a carpe diem practice her family uses. When they are having a good time together or enjoying the beauties of nature, one of her family members will say, "This is a good moment." It is a wonderful way to help everyone pause and appreciate what's happening around them.

12. Thank the cranks.

Chester's dad was once assigned to work with a group of boys in his church congregation and visibly enjoyed the work, but one woman must not have liked the bounce in his step and wanted to put him in his place. She said, "Brother Elton, you think all these youth love you, well I'm here to tell you they don't." Chester's dad said a quick thank-you. The woman was taken aback, and explained, "That wasn't a compliment." His response: "Too late." When we choose to rebuff negativity with gratitude, there's not much anyone can say.

13. Write letters of appreciation.
Whether you prefer handwritten missives or e-mails or social media posts, take time each week to write out a few notes of thanks to those who have influenced you. These letters may be directed to those who've helped you recently—a kid's teacher, the dry cleaner, or a favorite aunt who always makes time to babysit—or someone who influenced you in the past to whom you've never completely expressed your deep gratitude: a coach, teacher, mentor, parent, or friend. University of Michigan professor David Ulrich said his parents taught him the power of such letters of gratitude. "They each wrote gratitude notes to those who served them. One of the curses of our lives was buying dad a copy machine because he made copies of all his thank-you notes! Mom continues to write thank-you notes at age ninety."

AS WE CULTIVATE better relationships with our loved ones, we begin to better see them and value them. What do our kids and significant other laugh about? What sparks their passions? What are they working on? Observing and expressing gratitude to those we love is a critical component of loving relationships, with lessons learned that will help us on the job, too.

A wise man once said, "No other success can compensate for failure in the home." That's the beauty of gratitude. It isn't just for work; it affects all aspects of life.

Take It Home

- Some leaders give their best selves at work but have little left over for the people who should mean the most in their lives. And the opposite is just as common: Leaders are grateful, gracious, and respectful with friends and loved ones while ungrateful on the job.

- Research has shown that the power of keeping a daily gratitude journal is extraordinary. Studies show people are 25 percent happier if they keep gratitude journals. They also feel more energetic, are less envious, exercise more, and have lower blood pressure compared with people who do not keep these journals.

- Other ways to develop greater depths of gratitude in our personal lives include: Make a commitment to give undivided attention to your loved ones, be excited to see them, give immediate positive feedback to family members, be more grateful to your partner, be grateful for obstacles, teach your kids to give, serve together, and write letters of appreciation.

- As we cultivate better relationships with our loved ones with gratitude, we begin to better see them and value them. And the lessons learned will help us on the job, too.

Conclusion

One Giant Leap for Mankind

On July 20, 1969, when Neil Armstrong took his "one giant leap" onto the moon, he was clad in a custom-made spacesuit called an extravehicular mobility unit, or EMU for short. While to those watching on earth the suit seemed like a sturdy white tank, in truth there were just a few layers of synthetics, rubber, and metalized films separating him from the vacuum of space, solar radiation, and tiny meteorites hurtling through the void at thirty-six thousand miles an hour.

Leaving historic first footprints on the lunar surface, Armstrong moved freely. He collected priceless samples of lunar rocks and deployed scientific experiments. He even took an unplanned jog to photograph a crater about the distance of a soccer field from the lunar lander.

Armstrong was well aware that the care and effort put into the suit's design enabled him to return home safely. He later sent a letter of gratitude for his wearable "spacecraft" to the entire EMU team. He wrote of the suit, "It turned out to be one of the most widely photographed spacecraft in history, no doubt due to the fact that it was so photogenic." With typical self-deprecating humor, he added, "Equally responsible for its success was its characteristic of hiding from view its ugly occupant."

"Its true beauty, however," wrote the astronaut, "was that it worked."

Armstrong expressed his gratitude in a delightful way. If this tough-as-nails guy can do it, surely you can give it a try today.

The promise of this practice, according to professor and author Brené Brown, is a more joy-filled life. "The relationship between joy and gratitude was one of the important things I found in my research," she said. "I wasn't expecting it. In my twelve years of research on eleven thousand pieces of data, I did not interview one person who had described themselves as *joyful* who did not actively practice gratitude.

"It's not joy that makes us grateful," she sums up, "it's gratitude that makes us joyful."

Still, for some leaders, learning to practice the soft stuff like this might feel too mushy and touchy-feely. It might be tempting to tune it out as irrelevant to the bottom line, especially for those who need to hear it the most. But making human connections is our job as leaders, and helping employees feel valued and providing a little boost of joy at work can make a huge difference.

At least that's what Best Buy executive chairman Hubert Joly told us as we wrapped up our interview. As his head of communications was about to whisk him to another meeting, Joly paused and said, "If a CEO is grumpy, that becomes the acceptable attitude within the company. If you try to be positive, gracious, approachable, and grateful, it gets multiplied. In our case, by 125,000 people."

So we'll close the book with this challenge: Start small, start today. Choose just a few of the practices to focus on for a beginning and see how it goes. We are confident you'll see out-of-this-world results. That is our fondest hope for you, and for the people in your care.

We Are Grateful . . .

When we asked those we interviewed where they first learned to be grateful, most said from their parents. So we would be ungrateful louts if we did not first express gratitude to our parents: Joan and Gordon Gostick and Irene and Dalton Elton. Both couples made it magnificently through more than sixty years of married life and taught us early the value of a gracious thank-you. We are also eternally grateful to our clans: To Jennifer and Tony. And to Heidi and to Cassi and Braeden; Carter, Luisa, Lucas Chester, and Clara Iris; Brinden; and Garrett and Maile. There is no life of gratitude without those we love.

We offer deep thanks to our family at The Culture Works: Paul Yoachum, our marketing and strategy whiz; Lance Garvin, the master of sales who keeps us in the black; Christy Lawrence, our speaking agent extraordinaire; Chris Kendrick, who makes our clients feel like the most important people on the planet; Brianna Bateman, who keeps the TCW machine running; and Bryce Morgan, Asher Gunsay, Garrett Elton, Mark Durham, Jaren Durham, and the rest of The Culture Works team who help us serve our clients and build All In cultures every day.

We owe a debt of gratitude to our critical reader Emily Loose, who provided insights that made us look a lot smarter than we really are. We also thank Scott Christopher and Anthony Gostick for their reading and comments that contributed much to the final work.

Our agent Jim Levine has been as passionate about this project as we have been, and he lives a life of gratitude every day. Thank you, Jim, for believing in us and hauling us around New York City to find the right editor.

That editor is Hollis Heimbouch of HarperBusiness. She immediately got the idea and thought it had legs. Her energy, wit, and wisdom have been essential in guiding us in creating a book we are very proud of. We also thank her capable assistant Rebecca Raskin for her care in shepherding our manuscript to production.

To Mark Fortier, our publicist, and Brian Perrin of Harper-Business marketing, we express our appreciation for amplifying our message to the world.

To all those who are quoted herein, we are grateful for your brilliant minds and good hearts. We are better people because you are in our lives.

Finally, we express sincere appreciation to our friend Marshall Goldsmith and his COO, Sarah McArthur, for their contributions and support. This book began with a conversation with Marshall, and he has provided guidance and direction all the way. It's fair to say this book wouldn't exist without Marshall's help.

Notes

4 "at work than anyplace else": A finding culled from Amie Gordon, "Four Objections to Gratitude in the Workplace," *Greater Good Magazine* at UC Berkeley, November 8, 2017.

4 more grateful for their work: From Michael Schneider, "Employees Say This 1 Thing Would Make Them Work Harder (And 6 Reasons Why Managers Won't Do It)," *Inc.*, December 28, 2017.

4 is more likely to be successful.: The 96 and 94 percent statistics on bosses being more successful are from the research paper "Gratitude Survey—Conducted for the John Templeton Foundation," overseen by Janice Kaplan, June–October 2012. More than two thousand online surveys were completed.

5 one of the most famous quotes: Jerry Krause later said he was misquoted, and he claimed he had said "players and coaches alone do not win championships." Information on this story was obtained from Steve Rosenbloom, "Jerry Krause Deserved Better," *Chicago Tribune*, March 21, 2017; and Jack Silverstein, "The True Story of Jerry Krause and the Breakup of the Bulls," SBNation's *Blog a Bull*, March 24, 2017. https://www.blogabull .com/2017/3/24/15044772/the-true-story-of-jerry-krause-break up-of-the-bulls-michael-jordan-phil-jackson-scottie-pippen.

8 grateful managers lead teams: The two hundred thousand–person study was conducted for our book *The Carrot Principle*, Simon & Schuster/Free Press (2009).

9 An estimated $11 billion is lost in the United States: The $11 billion cost on employee turnover is according to Bryan Adams, "This Avoidable Situation Is Costing U.S. Businesses $11 Billion Every Single Year," *Inc.*, December 10, 2018.

9 the number one reason people give: The main cause of turnover, according to the U.S. Department of Labor, is a finding from Joe Facciolo, "4 Ways to Create an Impactful Employee Recognition Program," Rise People, August 3, 2017. https://risepeople.com/blog/create-an-impactful-employee-recognition-program/.

10 send a letter to someone they were grateful to: More information on the Kent State University study can be found in the Excellence in Action of that school's website and Emily Vincent, "Writing Power: Kent State University Professor Studies Benefits of Writing Gratitude Letters." http://einside.kent.edu/Management%20Update%20Archive/news/announcements/success/toepferwriting.html.

12 That is dubbed the negativity bias: Information on the negativity bias was influenced by Peter Diamandis, "Abundance—The Future Is Better Than You Think," found on the Singularity Hub, June 28, 2012. https://singularityhub.com/2012/06/28/abundance-the-future-is-better-than-you-think/.

14 can help people cope: Robert Emmons's groundbreaking work is part of the foundation all gratitude writers stand on. His quote comes from his article "How Gratitude Can Help You Through Hard Times," *Greater Good Magazine* at UC Berkeley, May 13, 2013.

14 we began to group together in communities: The nod to Adam Smith comes from Moya Sarner, "Is Gratitude the Secret of Happiness? I Spent a Month Finding Out," *Guardian*, October 23, 2018.

14 "failed to give credit where credit was due": The Florida State University study was noted in Sharon Perkins, "Top 5 Reasons Employees Hate Their Managers," in the Work-Life section of The Nest.

23 Fear at work is manifest in a myriad of ways: Our writings on fear were informed by Rachelle Williams, "What Is Fear? And How to Use It as Motivation," Chopra Center. https://chopra.com/articles/what-is-fear-and-how-to-use-it-as-motivation.

25 a culture of Total Quality Management: The Deming quote is fairly ubiquitous. We found it on "Driving Fear Out of Your Organization," Fearless Leaders Group. http://fearlessleaders group.com/driving-fear-out-of-your-organization.

25 work harder when their boss shows appreciation: The 81 percent statistic is from Michael Schneider, "Employees Say This 1 Thing Would Make Them Work Harder (And 6 Reasons Why Managers Won't Do It)," *Inc.*, December 28, 2017.

25 prompting the release of stress hormones: We better understood the stress response from "Understanding the Stress Response," on the Harvard Health Publishing website of Harvard Medical School, May 1, 2018. https://www.health.harvard.edu /staying-healthy/understanding-the-stress-response.

31 cultivating respect is more about love than fear: We shared the stage with Jake Wood at CHS in Las Vegas on March 4, 2019, and quote him from his talk.

33 the venerable American motor company: Most of the Alan Mulally information comes from our interviews with him, but analysis also came from Harry Kraemer, "How Ford CEO Alan Mullaly [sic] Turned a Broken Company into the Industry's Comeback Kid," *Quartz*, June 18, 2015.

39 employees would like more feedback: The finding that 65 percent of employees say they want more feedback is from Victor Lipman, "65% of Employees Want More Feedback (So Why Don't They Get It?)," *Forbes*, August 8, 2016.

39 says in this regard: Kris Duggan, "It's Time to End the Myth That Millennials Need Constant Praise," *Fortune*, February 7, 2017.

39 millennial blogger Kaytie Zimmerman: Kaytie Zimmerman is quoted from her article "What Every Manager Should Know about Recognizing their Millennial Employees," *Forbes*, October 22, 2017.

40 not solely the fault of young people: The facts on narcissism come partially from Joel Stein's *Time* magazine cover story "Millennials: The Me Me Me Generation," May 20, 2013.

40 overinflated view of how special their children are: We are quoting the Ohio State University/University of Amsterdam study that was written about by Alice Walton in "Too Much Praise Can Turn Kids into Narcissists, Study Suggests," *Forbes*, March 9, 2015. We also quote the study by Eddie Brummelman et al., "Origins of Narcissism in Children," *Proceedings of the National Academy of Sciences of the United States of America* 112, no. 12, March 9, 2015.

44 entirely different life before finding that quote: Brené Brown is quoted from Michelle Darrisaw, "Brené Brown's Netflix Special, *The Call to Courage*, Will Help You Access More Love, Joy, and Belonging," *O: The Oprah Magazine*, April 18, 2019.

45 some 98 percent of people say yes: Jim Kouzes and Barry Posner's book is *The Leadership Challenge*, 6th edition, Jossey-Bass (2017).

46 frequency of appreciation: Francesca Gino and Adam Grant spoke about the Wharton fundraising gratitude project to the *Harvard Business Review*'s IdeaCast, written up in *HBR* as "The Big Benefits of a Little Thanks," 2013.

46 John Gottman and Robert Levenson: We are quoting Gottman's work as best captured by Kyle Benson, "The Magic Relationship Ratio, According to Science," Gottman Project, October 4, 2017. https://www.gottman.com/blog/the-magic-relationship-ratio-according-science/.

50 one and a half to two times the employee's annual salary: The Deloitte data is from Josh Bersin, "Employee Retention Now a Big Issue: Why the Tide Has Turned," LinkedIn, August 16, 2013.

53 the financial performance their strategies promise: We are quoting Michael Mankins and Richard Steele from "Turning Great Strategy into Great Performance," *Harvard Business Review*, July–August 2005.

53 8 percent of an organization understands the strategy: Phil Jones's book is *Communicating Strategy*, Gower Publishing (2008).

54 helped change the company's entire strategy: We learned the

story of Patty McCord and the Netflix Culture Deck in her book *Powerful*, Silicon Guild (2018).

55 there is plenty of slack to pick up: Heike Bruch and Sumantra Ghoshal wrote about busy managers in "Beware the Busy Manager," *Harvard Business Review*, February 2002.

55 "instead of doing more things with side effects": Gary Keller's book is *The ONE Thing*, Bard Press (2013).

56 people who tend to be more or less grateful: We are quoting information on genes and brain activity from a few terrific articles: Summer Allen, "Why Is Gratitude So Hard for Some People?," May 10, 2018; and Adam Hoffman, "What Does a Grateful Brain Look Like?," November 16, 2015, both published in *Greater Good Magazine* at UC Berkeley. Dr. Jinping Liu is also quoted from the article by Summer Allen.

59 who follow the same route every day: Information on brain plasticity and London cabbies was gleaned from Pascale Michelon, "Brain Plasticity and How Learning Changes Your Brain," SharpBrains, February 26, 2008. https://sharpbrains.com/blog/2008/02/26/brain-plasticity-how-learning-changes-your-brain/.

60 "connecting different responses": Vanessa Loder is quoted from her article "How to Rewire Your Brain for Happiness," *Forbes*, March 18, 2015.

60 says Dr. Romeo Vitelli: Romeo Vitelli is quoted from his article "Hassles, Uplifts, and Growing Older," *Psychology Today*, June 9, 2014. He also provides information on brain plasticity from his article "Can You Change Your Personality?," *Psychology Today*, September 7, 2015.

61 daily changes in their behavior: Dr. Romeo Vitelli provides information on brain plasticity from his article, "Can You Change Your Personality?," *Psychology Today*, September 7, 2015.

62 act followed by a routine that creates a reward: Charles Duhigg's book is *The Power of Habit*, Random House (2012).

62 "the reward of a caffeine and sugar rush": Katherine Reynolds Lewis is quoted from "The Secrets to Habit Change," *Fortune*, April 16, 2015.

65 professors Amy Wrzesniewski and Jane Dutton: We quote the Michigan researchers' work from Schon Beechler, "Leadership Skills: Helping Others Find Meaning," *Forbes*, January 14, 2014.

67 typically come from 20 percent of "causes": We derived information on the Pareto Principle from "Understanding the Pareto Principle (The 80/20 Rule)," Better Explained. https://betterexplained.com/articles/understanding-the-pareto-principle-the-8020-rule/.

68 low-level job at the beginning of her working life: Schon Beechler is quoted from her article "The Role of Leaders in Helping Others Find Meaning at Work," on the INSEAD Leadership and Organisations blog, December 13, 2013. https://knowledge.insead.edu/blog/insead-blog/the-role-of-leaders-in-helping-others-find-meaning-at-work-3055.

72 "If it doesn't, people feel cheated": Bill Fotsch and John Case are quoted from their article "How to Build Incentive Plans that Actually Work," *Forbes*, August 24, 2015.

74 with attrition rates exceeding that of retail: The finding that technology is the industry with the greatest turnover comes from Paul Petrone, "See the Industries with the Highest Turnover (And Why It's So High)," LinkedIn, March 19, 2018.

75 far more motivating to employees: The German/Swiss study is quoted from Rebecca Hinds, "Google Made a Big Mistake with This Holiday Gift for Employees. Here's What Should Have Happened," *Inc.*, November 2018.

77 credit card accounts without their customers' knowledge: The information on Wells Fargo was quoted from Matthew Wisner, "Wells Fargo CEO on Account Scandal: We Had an Incentive Plan that Drove Inappropriate Behavior," Fox Business, September 13, 2017; and Max de Haldevang, "The Common Bonus Structures that Can Lead to Corporate Corruption Scandals," *Quartz*, October 24, 2017.

79 "possible outcome for that scenario": David Christopher Bell quipped in his article "The 14 Most Insane Ways Movie Char-

acters' Lives Changed Overnight," Film School Rejects. https://
filmschoolrejects.com/the-14-most-insane-ways-movie-characters
-lives-changed-overnight-4216b16ab766/.

80 personal humility and indomitable will: Jim Collins's book
is *Good to Great*, HarperBusiness (2001).

94 asking too many questions at once: We quote Hutch Carpenter on the over-ask from his article "Avoid These 3 Mistakes
When Asking for Employee Ideas," Hype, August 4, 2014.
https://blog.hypeinnovation.com/avoid-these-3-mistakes-when
-asking-for-employee-ideas.

96 492-bed Baptist Hospital in Pensacola, Florida: Quint Studer's
story was originally featured in our book *The Invisible Employee*,
Wiley (2009).

97 suggested by software engineer Charlie Ward: Ideas from
Amazon and British Airways were taken from Leila Durmaz,
"These 6 Ideas from Employee Suggestion Programs Boosted
Company Performance," April 12, 2013. http://imblog.ideaglow
.com/6-ideas-employee-suggestion-programs-boost-company/.

98 creates a virtuous circle: Alan Robinson and Dean Schroeder were quoted about Idemitsu from "Getting the Best Employee Ideas," *Harvard Business Review*, June 2004.

101 "assume positive intent": We quote Indra Nooyi from her
column "The Best Advice I Ever Got," *Fortune*, April 30, 2008.

108 "I was a raging bitch": Lynn Carnes was quoted from her
TED Talk "From Raging Bitch to Engaging Coach," October 19, 2015.

111 pick their CEO out of a lineup: The 2017 study that many
people don't know the CEO's name is from a survey and press
release from APPrise Mobile. The release is titled "America's
Invisible Bosses: Many U.S. Workers Don't Know their CEO's
Name or Face," April 26, 2017.

112 "I did housekeeping for a day": Tom Klein's story is quoted
from Catherine Hunter, "Case Study: Walk in Your Shoes,"
Smart Meetings, December 30, 2011. https://www.smartmeet
ings.com/magazine_article/case-study-walk-in-your-shoes.

113 "critical driver of overall performance" for managers: The data from DDI on only 40 percent of leaders being proficient in empathy is from Victor Lipman, "How Important Is Empathy to Successful Management?," *Forbes*, February 24, 2018.

119 it only took a few minutes: We quote Bryce Hoffman from his book *American Icon*, Crown Business (2012).

120 That term was made popular by Kim Scott: We quote Kim Scott on her concept of radical candor from Kim Bainbridge and Lisa Everson, "Radical Candor: Why Brutal Honesty Is Tech's Hottest Management Trend," NBC News Your Business, February 13, 2018. https://www.nbcnews.com/business/your-business/radical-candor-why-brutal-honesty-tech-s-hottest-management-trend-n842466.

126 creative breakthroughs in organizations: Teresa Amabile and Steven Kramer are quoted from their article "The Power of Small Wins," *Harvard Business Review*, May 2011.

130 one hundred–person team to come together: The SnackNation information comes from "12 Unique Examples of Employee Recognition in Action," Bonusly. https://bonus.ly/employee-recognition-guide/employee-recognition-examples.

131 the biggest obstacle to effectively serving their customers: The information that 70 percent of customer service professionals cite silos as the biggest problem is from "The Changing Role of the Modern Sales Team," SalesForce.com.

132 which encourages employees to present potential project ideas: The story of Frima Studios comes from Drew Gannon, "How to Reward Great Ideas," *Inc.*, July 19, 2011.

145 Harvard researcher Teresa Amabile and writer Steven Kramer: Teresa Amabile and Steven Kramer are quoted from their article "The Power of Small Wins," *Harvard Business Review*, May 2011.

148 New York state hospital to combat the problem: Tali Sharot's citation comes from her article "What Motivates Employees More: Rewards or Punishments?," *Harvard Business Review*, September 26, 2017.

149 The Gallup Organization data was cited in Jennifer Robison,

"In Praise of Praising Your Employees," Gallup, November 9, 2006. https://www.gallup.com/workplace/236951/praise-praising -employees.aspx.

151 gratitude should always include positive words: The Charles Schwab quote was found on goodreads.com.

163 3) platinum-level, and 4) diamond-level: An earlier version of these levels was outlined in our book *The Carrot Principle*, Simon & Schuster/Free Press (2009).

167 not only at work but in our personal lives: David Cherrington's account comes from his book *Rearing Responsible Children*, Bookcraft (1985).

170 technology company Button in New York City: The Button information comes from "12 Unique Examples of Employee Recognition in Action," Bonusly. https://bonus.ly/employee -recognition-guide/employee-recognition-examples.

171 vice president of sales at AddVenture Products: The account of AddVenture comes from Rebecca Hasting, "Personalized Recognition is Priceless," SHRM. https://www.shrm.org /resourcesandtools/hr-topics/employee-relations/pages/personal izedrecognitionis.aspx.

175 viewed tens of millions of times: Netflix's Culture Deck story is outlined in Patty McCord's book *Powerful*, Silicon Guild (2018), and can be found on the company website's culture page. https://jobs.netflix.com/culture.

178 according to a Johns Hopkins University study: The staggering 95 percent statistic is from Josh Bersin, "Culture: Why It's the Hottest Topic in Business Today," *Forbes*, March 13, 2015.

180 and nineteen values: Quicken Loans was noted from Wendell Robinson, "Quicken Loans: Culture Driven," *Training Industry*, summer 2016. https://trainingindustry.com/magazine /issue/quicken-loans-culture-driven/.

181 values of "accountability" and "excellence.": We learned of how accountability and excellence might conflict in "How to Resolve a Values Conflict," Ferguson Values, December 9, 2016. https://

www.fergusonvalues.com/2016/12/how-to-resolve-a-values
-conflict/.

189   Shawn Achor, author of *The Happiness Advantage*: Achor
is quoted from his article "The Benefits of Peer-to-Peer Praise
at Work," *Harvard Business Review*, February 19, 2016.

190   influence on employee engagement levels: The Simply Talent research is cited in "Peer-to-Peer Recognition," Workplace
Happiness, August 21, 2017, https://workplace-happiness.com
/2017/08/21/peer-to-peer-recognition/.

190   "Appreciation systems": The study on social recognition is
from the paper "Networks of Gratitude: Structures of Thanks
and User Expectations in Workplace Appreciation Systems" by
Emma Spiro, Nathan Matias, and Andrés Monroy-Hernández,
presented at the Tenth International AAAI Conference on
Web and Social Media, May 17–20, 2016.

193   "Networks of Gratitude: Structures of Thanks and User
Expectations in Workplace Appreciation Systems," by Emma
Spiro, Nathan Matias, and Andres Monroy-Hernandez, presented at the Tenth International AAAI Conference on Web
and Social Media, May 17–20, 2016.

194   celebrate other team members: The Bonusly information comes
from "12 Unique Examples of Employee Recognition in Action,"
Bonusly. https://bonus.ly/employee-recognition-guide/employee
-recognition-examples.

196   there are some practices to avoid: Peer-to-peer pitfalls to avoid
comes from Dave Zielinski, "Why Social Recognition Matters,"
SHRM, February 20, 2015. https://www.shrm.org/resource
sandtools/hr-topics/technology/pages/why-social-recognition
-matters.aspx.

197   they've done something noteworthy: The TypeForm information
comes from "12 Unique Examples of Employee Recognition in
Action," Bonusly. https://bonus.ly/employee-recognition-guide
/employee-recognition-examples.

197   senior director of customer service Rob Siefker: We originally

cited the Zappos story in our book *The Orange Revolution*, Simon & Schuster/Free Press (2010).

205 major turnaround in the life of one of her clients: Annie McKee is quoted from her article "If You Can't Empathize with Your Employees, You'd Better Learn To," *Harvard Business Review*, November 16, 2016.

208 more than two thousand people to show the value: Robert Emmons is quoted from Jessica Ravitz, "The Power of Gratitude, Year-Round Gift," CNN, November 26, 2009. http://www.cnn.com/2009/LIVING/11/25/giving.gratitude/index.html.

218 extravehicular mobility unit, or EMU for short: For the story of Neil Armstrong, we quote Andrew Chaikin, "Neil Armstrong's Spacesuit Was Made by a Bra Manufacturer," *Smithsonian Magazine*, November 2013.

219 is a more joy-filled life: Brené Brown is quoted from her article "Brené Brown on Joy and Gratitude," Global Leadership Network, November 21, 2018. https://globalleadership.org/articles/leading-yourself/brene-brown-on-joy-and-gratitude/.

Index

About the Gurus of Gratitude

ADRIAN GOSTICK is the coauthor of such books as *The Carrot Principle*, *The Best Team Wins*, and *All In*, which have been *New York Times* and number one *Wall Street Journal* bestsellers. His works have been translated into more than thirty languages and have sold 1.5 million copies around the world. He has appeared on NBC's *Today* show and been quoted in the *Economist*, *Harvard Business Review*, the *Wall Street Journal*, and *Fortune*. He is the cofounder of The Culture Works, a global firm focused on helping organizations attract, develop, and retain great people. Gostick is number three on the list of the Top 30 Global Gurus in Leadership and number nine in Organizational Culture. Learn more at adriangostick.com.

CHESTER ELTON'S work is supported by research with more than one million working adults. He has been called the "apostle of appreciation" by Canada's *Globe and Mail*, "creative and refreshing" by the *New York Times*, and a "must read for modern managers" by CNN. Elton is coauthor of *The Carrot Principle*, *The Best Team Wins*, and *All In* and has been quoted in publications such as the *Wall Street Journal*, the *Washington Post*, and *Fast Company*. A sought-after lecturer around the world, he is ranked by Global Gurus as number eight in Organizational Culture and number eleven in Leadership. He is cofounder of The Culture Works, and more than seven hundred thousand people follow his work on LinkedIn. Learn more at chesterelton.com.

About The Culture Works

ADRIAN GOSTICK AND CHESTER ELTON are founders of The Culture Works,® a firm dedicated to creating All In Cultures.™ The organization is home to What Motivates Me Engagement Training, All In Culture Training, Best Team Wins Teamwork Training, and Leading with Gratitude Training. The Culture Works is also the provider of the Motivators Assessment™— the world's most extensive scientific assessment to help individuals identify their unique blend of core motivators. Based on two decades of experience and the results of workplace interviews with more than one million adults, the company's research-based training programs and *New York Times* best-selling books help create cultures that attract, develop, and retain great talent. Learn more at TheCultureWorks.com.